THE SATISFACTION OF SURRENDER

God's personalized pursuit of our attention

Megan J. Marasigan

Copyright © 2020 Megan J. Marasigan

All rights reserved

Bible references quoted from ESV. NIV, HCS

No part of this book may be reproduced, or stored in a retrieval system, or transmitted in any form or by any means, electronic, mechanical, photocopying, recording, or otherwise, without express written permission of the publisher.

"Turn your eyes upon Jesus"
Copyright: Public Domain
Author: Helen Howarth Lemmel (1922)

Cover design by: Author through www.Cava.com
Library of Congress Control Number: TBA
Printed in the United States of America

To Micah, Emma, Mom, Dad, Lara and my closest friends. A little crazy, a lot of Jesus, and all of your support goes a long way. Love you.

CONTENTS

Title Page	1
Copyright	2
Dedication	3
Introduction	7
The Satisfaction of Surrender	11
Chapter 1	13
Chapter 2	26
Chapter 3	36
Chapter 4	45
Chapter 5	56
Chapter 6	65
Chapter 7	73
Chapter 8	84
Chapter 9	93
Chapter 10	102
About The Author	109

INTRODUCTION

The Satisfaction Of Surrender

by Megan J. Marasigan

Staring at these words scrawled across the page, I can't help but be flattened by the humility required to write even a paragraph about the deep and wide subject of surrender, let alone a book. I want you to know that before I even began to research or outline a chapter, I had to spend time in prayer and worship with my Savior. I say "I had to" not because anyone was forcing me to, but because what I have found out repeatedly in my life is that the result of anything done through my own vision and efforts, pales in comparison with anything I do through Him. Though pieces of this book give some insight into my story, that story is not mine to share. It is His, and my prayer is that I get out of the way. That is part of my surrender process, and, really, it is part of yours too.

I wonder what this moment in your life looks like for you right now. This second, I wonder what your heart is needing. Are you the one staring at the bottom of the pit you are in? Is that pit very real for you, and does the light you pray for seem to be hiding from you? Or are you the one who knew that nightmarish season years ago when you woke up and reached for breath, and somehow, someway, it's no longer your day-to-day reality? Perhaps you are the reader who knows people within your life who have suffered greatly, but you can honestly say in comparison that you have not. Do you wonder why they suffer, and you do not? Do you wonder if that will ever be you? Do you pray it won't be?

Friends, I was all of the above. I am all of the above. But, before I go any further into even touching on the broken and the resurrected parts of my story, I cannot delay in turning our current moment together toward the real and powerful hope that is in our Savior, Jesus Christ. Within the entire Bible, an intentional stream that weaves its way through every marking on every page demands that our attention is turned to the One who loves us with His whole being, the One who surrendered His throne because of that love. That love gently and personally bades us to surrender to it too. At no point in that marvelous book was there a ball dropped in that purpose. Every joy. Every suffering. Every praise and cry. Every person and place. Every moment is designed to point us to a Savior who knows us at a cellular level. He KNEW us when those words were written. He KNEW us when the moments took place in real time. We were on His mind and written on His heart even as he watched Moses being placed in the floating basket, when David plotted to kill Bathsheba's husband, when the brave young boys were placed into the hot furnace, and Paul gave praise in prison as the doors flew open…. God was thinking of YOU.

He already knew YOUR story and mine. He already knew your deepest desires and struggles as well as your beautiful potential. He knew what it would take to reach that potential. But he also knew He couldn't eternally enjoy the unique creation that you are without getting your attention in unique ways.

Oh, how He must wish that our attention would be forever captured in more simple moments. Like that childhood moment when you noticed the detail in the butterfly's wing, or the split second when you saw the star shoot across the sky and realized how small you are, or you heard your baby's heartbeat knowing you had nothing to do with its first flutter. And what about that event that you couldn't explain, that one moment in your life that pointed to someone else protecting or guiding you, and you knew there was something bigger out there?

I wonder how many times God has tried to turn my attention by more simple means and I never noticed or eventually became distracted. The depths and the sacrificial lengths to which my Father goes to continue to capture my heart! There were intense moments when His presence and His character were so vivid and full like a bursting sunrise of majestic color, and others when it came in fleeting whispers of minute detail like the butterfly's wing. On one hand, I desperately wish all it took was the memory of the soft blades of grass I laid on while staring at the cloud shapes. I wish that was the second it all clicked for me and I knew Him like He wants me to and surrendered my whole being to Him because of that second of smallness. Yet, on the other hand, it has been the vast collection of individualized moments in my life that have repeatedly been pierced with His consistent love for me, and I am thoroughly aware that every volume and chapter of that story is how I got to know and treasure His love.

My goal with this book is not for you to identify with my story. I did add pieces of my life to each chapter, but more so, I want you to be able to reflect on how the truths in each chapter can be applied to your story. I have included poignant Biblical connections at the end of each chapter that will help you apply and solidify the truths in this book. Don't miss out on these. Consider them the bow that ties up the purpose of each chapter. I urge you to have your Bible with you throughout this book, jot notes, highlight, and engage when something hits home with you.

These are those personal and unique moments of which I speak. Notice how He draws us to surrender through different themes in our lives. How does He draw you in personalized ways to Him in surrender? You don't need to walk in my shoes to relate. My hope is for you to recognize the abiding love stream within each chapter that points to the One who knew how and when to reveal Himself to you in the ways that would indeed uniquely capture your attention. My prayer is that you can see how personalized your sanctification process is within your own story. He knew when and how to touch your life. He knows that your surrendering comes through a litany of small and large moments of pain and joy. Your sanctification is a love story of your surrender that He has been writing forever.

THE SATISFACTION OF SURRENDER

Chapter 1. Control to surrender

Chapter 2. Sickness to surrender

Chapter 3. Loss to surrender

Chapter 4. Injury to surrender

Chapter 5. Sin to surrender

Chapter 6. Wrestling to surrender

Chapter 7. Dependence to surrender

Chapter 8. Waiting to surrender

Chapter 9. Heart to surrender

Chapter 10. Satisfaction of surrender

CHAPTER 1

Control to Surrender

Any comfort we seek above the Comforter will eventually lose its ability to comfort.

I'm not sure if tossing a coin is a great way to choose the title of a chapter, but when two options are just too equal in truth and meaning, you flip over the couch cushions! A dusty nickel decided on the word *control,* but its close cousin *comfort* is often the more palatable choice.

I think the nickel was right though. I'll explain. Humans are comfort creatures for sure. We love our buttered and battered foods, our soft blankets, and perfect temp A/C. We shove inserts into our sneakers that cost nearly as much as our shoes and we send back our food when it's a tad too cold. I do enjoy light ice in my cherry soda, and in our house, no one is happy when we order pizza because someone is always disappointed about the depth of the crust. And who doesn't appreciate the convenience of an elevator when lugging heavy suitcases or if there is a toddler in tow?

We all seek comfort, but what the proverbial flipped coin knew was when we say comfort, we really mean control.

Control is a nasty word. I don't think most people like to be considered controlling. When I ponder examples of controlling qualities, I think of types from the Myers Briggs personality test or the recently popular Enneagram. I can picture a few tightly wound bosses who certainly fit in the Type A category. The cartoon wife that nags or the overworked husband complaining about the burnt chicken fit into the judge-worthy cliche'. Those controlling figures aren't exactly something to which we aspire.

Control has a reputation. People get out of the way to avoid its shrapnel. But comfort? No, comfort is benign. Who can blame us for wanting to be comfortable? Afterall, we have designed our world for comfort! I can sit in my jammies and order clothes online (after checking out all the reviews of course because Heaven forbid the item I want has less than 4.5 stars) and eagerly anticipate the arrival of that brown smiling box. I can try on my clothes in the comfort of my own bedroom with my own lighting and my own mirror. If I am not fully satisfied, I just drop my order off at one of an array of locations to send it back and not even pay for shipping. How comfortable.

I've got the world's music in my pocket this second. I don't need a wall-to-wall bookshelf of CDs anymore. My groceries are delivered. My floors get swept by a little, round robot, and I can literally purchase a car online without getting out of my recliner. How comfortable.

Feel badly yet? Truly, that is not my goal here. For goodness sake, I am in that aforementioned recliner right now! Comfort isn't the enemy, but it is all too often a careful disguise. An ingrained distraction. We would rather look at the disguise because it is far more pleasant and accepted than the potentially hideous face behind it.

Control.

Our desire for comfort can become a mindset. A habit. It can begin as a justified means of enjoyment and become minimized in a way that we cannot see it grow into a lifestyle of expectation of that comfort. What once was a child's innocent preference for no ketchup on his hotdog becomes, with repetition, a now hamster-wheel of life decision-making dedicated to controlling his own personalized comfort at all costs. This is where the danger sets in. We choose the college that is the closest or farthest, or the mate that currently brings us the comfort of happiness and looks good on our arms. We choose the houses in the right school districts for the comfort of our children's similar socio-economic friend choices or the job that provides us with the comfortable lifestyle we envision, and so on. Again, it is not that these goals are sinful, but it begs to ask who is in charge of our hearts when setting them.

The Bible is full of people struggling to give up control. Actually, everyone was! Remember the rich young ruler in the book of Mark, chapter 10? He desired eternal life, but when Jesus told him to sell everything, give it to the poor, and then follow Him. The young man sadly went away because great were his possessions. We are going to dive deeper into this later, but I want to point out that this was not just about possessions. Possessions give us something we really want; comfort. Without those earthly things, from where would comfort come?

All too often when I am seeking comfort, the silent engine running the show behind the curtain is admittedly control or more specifically, the fear of giving up control. Yes, I wish to control my food, the quality of what I spend my money on, my mattress firmness, and the outcome of all daily decisions I make. This isn't something I can just turn off through any human capacity. It is not natural to desire to be uncomfortable.

Discomfort isn't the goal either.

Then what is the goal? My friends, I believe the goal is ultimately surrender. There are a lot of ways to think about surrender, and surrender doesn't always mean discomfort. Read the examples below and ask yourself whether you think of surrender in a negative or positive light in each one.

1. The soldier waving the white flag to concede the battle
2. The first "I love you".

3. The baby's cries slowly dwindling down as she falls asleep
4. The "hands up" thief caught red-handed with the police flashlight in his eyes.
5. The parachute-strapped skydiver's first step out of the airplane
6. The last breath of the weary, aged patriarch, his bed surrounded by loved ones
7. The moment you hit "send" when emailing a resume
8. The last document signature when a house is being sold
9. The father giving his daughter's hand away in marriage
10. The summer camp trust fall

Whatever these examples or some of your own bring to mind, one thing they have in common is that giving up control in the moment opens up the potential of the unknown. And that makes us feel uncomfortable.

Vulnerable.

Isn't that what we really fear? We like to control what comes next because that helps us reach a comfortable state. The unknown can be paralyzing! What will happen when the soldier is then captured? At least on the while still on the battlefield he still had a gun and was surrounded by his own people. How about the "L" word taking its first risk of rejection, or the father giving his daughter away praying the man she chose will care for her and love her through the years of the unknown. Even the summer camp trust fall is meant to show a young person that giving up control/fear of being dropped is worth the relief of being caught. Surrender.

What will happen next?
What will make me happy and comfortable?

What will cause me pain or discomfort?

What.

We have this all wrong. At least I did. Comfort is all about focusing on ourselves and the "what" that makes us comfortable. But surrender teaches us to focus our trust on the "Who" with a capital W. It's not the "what" that changes us and gives us true comfort that lasts. It is the "Who".

2 Corinthians 1:5 says, "For just as we share abundantly in the sufferings of Christ, so also our comfort abounds through Christ."

Our comfort abounds through Christ. Abounds! There are verses upon verses that point to God as our source of comfort. The Bible even names Him "Our Comforter". I love the beautiful fact that over and over again "what" we need is in our "Who" and we can call Him by name. He is our hope on the otherside of our surrender!

Surrendering control need not be this terrible thing we fear. It is actually an exchange, and we receive the advantage! We hand over this worthless, temporary and ultimately unsatisfying hamster-wheel-of-comfort and receive an eternally thirst-quenching *Comforter.* If we could only see the benefit of the exchange rate! We are not the source of our comfort and will never really find the "what" that will satisfy, but it takes time and repetition to grasp the reality of this truth.

The hymnist Helen H. Lemmel got it right when she wrote *"Turn your eyes upon Jesus. Look full in His wonderful face; and all the things of earth will grow strangely dim in the light of His glory and grace."*

Have you ever had a craving for a particular flavor of ice cream? Maybe you can think of one right now. In that craving moment the feeling is so sure. That flavor is just what will satisfy. You can almost taste it when you think about it. Yet, when you get to the counter and see the variety of other options, your original craving isn't the only driving force now. Suddenly, there is a shift you weren't expecting. The initial craving doesn't go away, but it no longer takes up the entirety of your tastebud desires. As a matter of fact, you begin to think you might experience regret if you don't consider your other options. Then, there is the moment when the temptation of getting 2 scoops of 2 different flavors rings like a Hallelujah chorus or a wrestling match "ding", and that is your answer. You get it all!

But how did this happen? Just minutes ago, you were perfectly satisfied with the thought of the one flavor, and had it magically appeared in your hand, you probably wouldn't have had a second thought of another flavor option.

Now, admittedly this example sounds trite, but it illustrates that your mind's ability to truly know what will satisfy your desires for comfort is far less accurate and concrete than we feel in the moment. The craving to satisfy and control our comfort levels can be quite loud at first, whether it's ice cream choices, house hunting, a new relationship etc. What we think we want isn't trustworthy. It's surprisingly and even dangerously fickle.

This can be a bad thing, sure, but I actually think it is a blessing if God gets a hold of our "comfort meter". When we fix our eyes on Jesus, what the hymn says is absolutely true. The things of earth, the ever-fickle comforts of our human flesh, begin to grow strangely dim *in comparison* to His glory and grace. A new comfort shift happens, but to a Source far more satisfying. Our very own desires for the "what" begin to transform to the desire for the

"Who". Once we experience this with repetition, that is when we begin to see the benefit of surrendering the control of our comfort.

These changes in our desires begin in small ways, however. The sanctification process of surrendering takes a lifetime of shifting our perspectives and giving Him control. As He proves Himself satisafactory, it gets easier in many ways.

God wants to be engaged with us in everything. Some say, "the devil is in the details". Maybe. But, in my experience, God loves us so much that He is the one who delights in the smallest of moments with us.

[31] *Therefore, whether you eat or drink, or whatever you do, do everything for God's glory.* 1 Corinthians 10:31

Am I reaching too far here? I don't think so. Look at 1 Corinthians 10:31 above. Paul didn't make any sort of mistake here in mentioning the regular, daily repetition of eating and drinking. Instead, he begins with that and then adds "whatever you do" and then "do everything" for Whose purpose? God's glory. The Who. Our Comforter

How is giving Him control in all things, like eating and drinking, or choosing a dentist for that matter, connected with God's glory? It's all about surrendering our very purpose here on earth. The choices simply aren't your choices to make alone, and you certainly do not control the outcome of those choices. You were MADE for God's glory. It is the reason for each heartbeat and breath. Simply being alive and reading this page has one ultimate purpose: God's glory.

Honestly, this concept is so big that it's hard to swallow. Am

I really supposed to be able to surrender every moment to be sure I am always giving God glory?

Every second?

I think we both understand that this concept is impossible. On this side of eternity, it *is* impossible, and that is why this chapter is all about control leading us to surrender.

Not only are we not in control, we aren't even in control of us fully giving up control! A major step in surrendering control is the realization that we don't actually have it to begin with. We never did, and we never will. Control is a lie.

We. Need. Him.

Our smallness should lead us to the bigness of God's complete and total control of all things; even our ability to let go. Though I have free will, I am utterly relying on Him down to every single second and I am fooling myself when I think differently. But, this is not a loss. This is a gain!

This realization of my utter dependence on Him did not even spark until much later in my life. I hate to think that I thought I deserved things like college, marriage, children, a house etc. I probably never really realized that I felt I deserved these things as much as I just looked at them as normal things to expect. I went to a small school through high school and I dated a little. I wasn't very worldly growing up. My first real head-on collision with the real world was when I started working at 15 years old. Through a series of events, I met a guy, and through another series of events we started dating. He wasn't a Christian and honestly, it didn't faze me much. What I now understand is that although I grew up in church, I had a low-grade quality of spiritual head knowledge that had not yet reached my heart. The concepts of inviting God to guide me and surrendering my decisions in dating or much else weren't blips on my radar. I had no fear of the outcome mostly because I didn't put a lot of thought into it. I glided and drifted from one day to the next with an immature assumption of a protective bubble around me, similar to how many youths do.

When I started this relationship, I had already been accepted into a college out of state. I made it clear that I wasn't changing my plans, but we continued dating. A few months later I was unpacking my car to take my items into my dorm room; carrying with me an attachment to a hometown boyfriend several states away. He stuck around via expensive phone bills and periodic visits. We dated long-distance until I finished school three and a half years later. I was then re-packing my car to return to Florida and marry him.

I condensed what is clearly a more detailed story because I am so eager to return to the beginning points of this chapter. I could within reason blame ignorance and youth and young love for my decision making. It would all be valid. I was young. I was excited to go away to college and thrilled my boyfriend stuck through several years of dating from miles and miles away. How romantic! I couldn't pass a bookstore without running in to grab the next issue of a wedding magazine and "dogear" ideas! When it came time to get married, I pushed away thoughts of doubt. There was no room for that in my bibble. This was the next step in a series of steps I had taken, and it was logical to take one more. That one more step turned into many, many more and soon we were building a house, working, and going to graduate school. We were comfortable making these choices. Completely comfortable.

Now, don't misunderstand what I share as a bunch of whiny regrets. I'm a few decades past these choices and have the luxury of seeing the beauty God intricately made out of my false sense of control. I know now how incredible it is when decisions are placed at His feet wrapped in surrender. I can't help but wonder what I would have done differently if the comfortable choices weren't the steps I took. I can't help but wonder what would have happened if I had recognized that comfort wasn't the goal. What would have happened if I had realized the significance of something so small as my heart beating silently for His glory and compared that to the importance of surrendering my college, marriage, and future choices to the purpose of bringing Him glory?

You see, I wasn't created to choose a college or a spouse. I wasn't created to experience dorm life or build a house. And neither were you. We were created so that everything we do, from seemingly insignificant to radically life-altering, is for the sole purpose of bringing Him glory. Not bringing us comfort.

So, who is held responsible for my not understanding that as a young person? Do I get to claim ignorance? Sure, there are natural consequences that result in every decision we make. Whether you are out for comfort or blatant control, our decisions do have consequences even if we don't notice the connection. I did experience consequences. Some wonderful, and some quite terrible. Some consequences I am still experiencing even now. But who is held responsible for my ignorance of the ultimate purpose of my existence?

Me? *It should be.*

But No. Not me.

Jesus.

His death shouted our purpose! If our purpose is not comfort or control, but that everything we are and do is for God's glory in response to His sacrificial love for us, then Jesus's death is not just covering our sin; it is covering our ignorance, as well as our human inability to fully surrender. It is impossible for us to stop and give God the glory for each heartbeat. We are humanly incapable of dedicating our microseconds to His glory one by one, but through Him every intentional and unintentional failure is covered! The Bible calls that willful and un-willful sin. It covers what I *cannot* do and what I can, but *choose* not to, do.

Praise Him!

Jesus surrendered His throne to present you blameless and

totally surrendered to His Father for God's glory, and you are now justified through Him. Surrendering our comfort and ultimately our control of our existence is a process of sanctification that will not be complete until we are at His throne. This process slowly removes the need to be comfortable and in control and then it replaces that desire with the gratification of the knowledge that He is in control of all things. Take joy in this! Allow relief to cover you! The striving can cease. No longer do we have to exhaust ourselves with the constant seeking of comfort. We can let out our held breath and rejoice in surrendering the outcome of every moment because it was never in our hands. The empty grip can be unclenched. We can know that whatever we learn and experience in each decision will be tailored to knowing Him better. The better we know Him, the more closely our decisions are aligned with Him. That right there is far better than comfort or control. That right there is a new kind of surrender.

Read Mark 10:17-22

The rich young ruler clearly saw something in Jesus. Maybe he watched Jesus perform miracles. Maybe he heard Jesus speak.
What did the man call Jesus? "Good…_____"

Fill in the blanks when he said. "what must_____ _____?"

What was the ultimate comfort that he desired? _____

Was this man wanting a "Who" or a "What"? _____

Jesus addressed each misunderstanding hidden in the man's question. He asked the man "Why do you call me good? No one is good other than God alone."

So, by asking this, what was Jesus revealing to the man about *Who* Jesus actually was? Was He just a teacher? No. He was _____

Yes. This man needed to see that Jesus was God! I can picture Jesus shaking His head.

Next, Jesus asked the young man if he had kept the commandments. But notice Jesus only mentioned commandments concerning sin against man.

Look at Exodus 20 and list the commandments Jesus didn't mention to the man.
_____
_____
_____

What was Jesus subtly pointing out that the man was missing out on?

_____

Yes! The young man spent his life doing good, having good intentions, and eventually accumulating a comfortable lifestyle. By all means this was a decent human being with an earned, respected reputation. If there was a "good guy" checklist, he would probably be the name at the top.

Then, how did Jesus look at the man? _____

What did Jesus ask the man to do? Sell _____ and give to_____. Then you will have treasures where?_____

I used to think this was unfair. I felt sorry for the man because to me, it seemed he was doing nothing wrong. He was an example of capitalism and community at its best. Couldn't he follow Jesus in his heart without selling everything and leaving his life behind? But, that is the point Jesus was making. It's all about the *willingness* to surrender. Only after surrendering the control and desire for the comforts of this earth would Jesus have him to follow Him. Let me rephrase that. Jesus knew that this man could not in his own human ability follow Him until he was willing to let go of the grip of comfort in his life. Not just the comfort --the grip it had on his focus and his heart.

Whether your comfort is connected to possessions, goals, dreams, or cravings.... it's the heart's focus that matters.

Look at Matthew 6: 19-24. What does verse 21 say?
_____
_____

Where is your comfort coming from these days? Is it regularly a "what" or a "Who"? Take a minute to talk to God about this. Ask Him to give you the desire to crave Him over your plans, your comforts, your fears of the unknown, and anything else that is derailing surrendering control. Write your prayer here and use it to remind yourself of the Who.

_____
_____
_____
_____

CHAPTER 2
Sickness to Surrender

The wonders of God will always pull us out of the shadows of our brokenness.

I totally botched my college GPA when I decided to take some courses out of interest and not necessity. For example, I was signing up for summer classes and I needed a few electives. The summer options were pretty sparse. I do remember badminton being one of the choices. Now, I like badminton, but I have this annoying predisposition to challenge myself. Although I was majoring in the English education field, I had always had an interest in how the human body works. Mind you, interest doesn't always translate to ability. I got through my high school science classes with decent grades, but when I chose to take college level Anatomy as an elective, I was under no thoughts of grandeur that I would do very well. Still, the curiosity outweighed the inevitable lower-than-normal grade that I would most likely earn.

I loved that class. I skated out of there with a proud C+ and my desire to fill my curiosity was not disappointed. The only C's I ever got were in that class and Spanish, but to me, it was worth it. I've often wondered where my interest in the human body came from. The only thing I can connect is an experience when I was 15. While on a packed bus to a church camp, I experienced incredibly sharp pains in my right side. It came on quite fast. My face turned green, I'm told, and my mind was filled with panic. I was imagining the horrid scene from the movie *Aliens* based on the splitting pain I was experiencing. By the end of the day, I had been rushed back home, tortured with an obscene number of tests at the ER, and later I found myself sitting in front of my family doctor. There was a large mass within my belly that had at some point pushed onto my kidney. My kidney rejected this invader by a series of pain signals, hence my greenish face. There was also a smaller mass around my reproductive organs that needed attention as well. They wouldn't know much more until they opened me up.

The next day, I had a 9" vertical scar on my stomach that looked like a long, stapled worm. The masses were removed, and the doctor was explaining that these were ovarian eggs that had continued to grow into benign tumors. Thankfully they were not cancer, but they clearly wreaked havoc on my body. He suggested to my mother that in the future I might experience some reproductive problems, but that it would be hard to know that now. At 15, all I was thinking about was how difficult it would be to find a bathing suit that would cover the scar. I think back to this time and I'm ashamed that it didn't rattle me more.

It was 8 years later that my husband and I were sitting on the other side of yet another doctor's desk hearing words I was having a hard time processing. "Your tests show that your chances of conceiving are very low. Almost zero. If conception were to occur with the assistance of medications or IVF, your chances of carrying a child to term is even lower." Apparently, the hormones needed to conceive, and another set of hormones needed to create a safe environment for any potential baby, were on permanent strike. I honestly do not remember being very emotional. I think denial or simple shock is probably more accurate. I was still in my bubble.

As mentioned in previous paragraphs, I am by nature a pretty determined person. I don't like to concede defeat. Coupled with a growing faith that I was experiencing at this time in my life, the idea of never having children of my own felt like a diagnosis that wasn't for me.

A quick fix. That is what I was after. Take the meds. Time everything out. Check off the health and nutrition boxes, tag the bases, and believe God would provide. Believe. Faith is a beautiful thing, but I simplified this situation as though God and I were teaming up. I thought, "You do Your part, and I'll do mine, and together we will solve this problem".

How arrogant.

I wish this part of the story was all about my strong surrendered faith and hours wearing out the "knees" of my jeans in prayer. It's not. I was still struggling with controlling the outcome, even when it came to the function of my own body and the creation of life.

After 2 years of little progress, including a painful miscarriage, strain on my marriage, and no light at the end of this dark tunnel, I found myself in a broken and grossly hopeless state. In our society, we grip onto the rights of our healthy bodies as though they are something we have earned and deserve. It seems like a personal insult when our bodies don't function perfectly. Tragedy and trauma around us certainly affect us greatly, but experiencing bodily pain or physical brokenness seems to turn everything upside-down like nothing else can. It did for me. I think this was the moment my eyes started to open up and not only see, but accept, my smallness.

Here's a Christian truth bomb. I have never enjoyed hearing about the story of Job. I have a feeling I am not the only one. Whether it's the difficulty in understanding the permission God gave Satan to attack Job's life, the not-so-great friends he had, the many chapters of Job's lamenting, or facing the fear of simply not wanting to be in his shoes in any way; it's a tough book to read.

Are you with me on this?

Yet, there is a richness in Job's story that I had let be overshadowed by the above. I'd like to show you. Would you take a minute to pray for God to open your heart to this precious book?

Please read Job chapter 1.

In chapter 1, Job experienced incredible calamity and unexplainable loss. External loss. One after another. Words had not fully come out of his mouth when more and more traumatic news unrelentingly continued coming.

Once he was able to respond, his words were this, *"Naked I come from my mother's womb, and naked I will leave this life. The Lord gives, and the Lord takes away. Blessed be the name of the Lord."* (Job 1:21)

He had torn his robe, shaved his head, and fell to the ground worshiping. He did not sin or blame God for anything. I want us to pause here to grasp this. Incredible. Nearly everything he loved, protected, purified, and worked for in his life had been ripped from him in violent and horrific ways. The bodies were still warm on the ground; his own children. Smoke was still in his nostrils. This wasn't a horror movie scene. It was real. Yet, his response, though in utter grief, was to worship, bless, and not sin or even blame the Lord.

Let's pause now to read Chapter 2. Here's what I really want us to weigh in on.

Something quite revealing of our human nature occurs in chapter 2 that creates a massive shift that is worth noticing. Satan tells God in chapter 2 that a man will give up everything in exchange for his *own life*. He then strikes Job's body with infected boils from the soles of his feet to the top of his head. Not just boils; infected boils. Allow your mind to bring up this immagery. This kind of infection comes with fever, lethargy, oozing, itching, stench, and misery.

The passage states that although his wife questioned if he was going to continue holding onto his integrity and she suggested he curse God and die (I assume to cease the suffering), Job did not sin.

Job did not sin.

He did not fall down and worship this time, but he did not sin. How many times have we struggled to worship? When our minds are troubled, it's hard to lift our voices in praise to Him. But, what about when our bodies are broken and in pain? Have you found that it's even harder? It seems that Job did. He had worshiped when his possessions and his children were destroyed, but there is no immediate mention of worship when he became overcome with sickness.

Physical sickness trauma attacks us in ways that are very different than trauma outside our body like Job's first wave of suffering. Not necessarily less or more severe, but different. Both affect us mentally, emotionally, spiritually, and physically, but still differently. When our bodies are afflicted, it's very personal. In my experience, it's almost offensive.

Personal sickness is something we can't get away from. It goes with us everywhere. When we eat, sleep, wake, travel, work; always. It is a constant. It is exhausting. It plays tricks on our wakeful thinking, and on our rest. It is a drain on every facility and, if left unsurrendered, can pull us into a dangerous and hopeless darkness. We can battle an emotion and even conquer it, but no matter how hard we try, we can't heal ourselves or force our bodies to feel better.

In chapter 6, verse 11, Job asks *"What strength do I have that I should continue to hope?"* Job didn't complain and question God in chapter 1, even while he was deeply grieving. It was when his body was attacked and he was suffering in personal and physical pain that he couldn't continue to function or push through. It stopped him in his tracks -- literally. Can you imagine infected sores on the soles of your feet? As a teacher, I have dealt with plantar fasciitis, and just that small pain altered my day even in big ways. I'd limit my need to walk as much as I could to avoid the pain. It's hard to imagine trying to do anything with my entire body covered in boils. I am actually impressed that Job could muster chapter after chapter of complaining and questioning God, or the company of such wishy-washy friends! Bodily pain and brokenness can make people feel like they are trapped! Desperate.

Sickness truly reveals our fragility and weakness. While trying to overcome the barriers of fertility issues I eventually faced how fragile my body was. No matter what I did to make myself function correctly, I was ultimately humbled by my weak and limited human state. I can relate to Job mentioning hope because hope in God's power was really all I had left.

Hope can be exhausting, and that is really because it's a daily choice to surrender the healing outcome. Hope requires fighting yourself from taking back the false control. In my case and in Job's, it was a daily choice to surrender to the truth of God's utter control of our bodies.

It's hard for us to wrap our brains around God allowing us to get sick. We know that sickness is connected to the original sin and it is easy for us to quickly begin to wonder if we get sick because we have recently or are presently doing something wrong. In my case, I wondered that for sure. I don't think that I was wanting to know this answer because I desired to be right with God. I thought that if I nailed down which sin I committed and asked for forgiveness, then maybe He'd heal me and then, frankly, I would get what I wanted. That's a pretty big confession right there, but it's very human to think and a human heart to have.

Job wondered the same. In chapter 7, verse 20 Job says, "*If I have sinned, what have I done to you? Watcher of humanity? Why have you made me your target? So that I have become a burden to you?*"

We all want to know why we suffer physically. God has given us this internal eternal drive for a perfect world and that includes a perfect body. Someday we will experience that fully, so it's difficult sometimes for us to accept that this is not possible during our earthly time here. Yet, we expect and demand it and we are shocked when we don't get it. So, we want to fix it. We search for sin that caused it and worry that it will be our own ignorance of our failures that will prevent our healing! Doesn't this sound more like a heart issue? I see some control in their rather than a humility leading us to confess unrepented sin.

Yes, there are consequences to a world of sin, and sickness can be connected to that, but what is driving that repentance? Reconciliation with God? Cleansing of unrighteousness? Continued sanctification? Or feeling better?

Job had asked why God made him a target. My heart is saddened by these words. We gravely misunderstand what God can do with pain and, even worse, we misunderstand the heart of our Father. He takes no pleasure in our pain or suffering. Jesus knows suffering firsthand. We have confidence that He understands it well. But suffering is never used simply for the purpose of punishment and consequence. If we are experiencing consequence, it is never the only purpose and certainly never the most important by far. God is in the business of restoring our souls through our surrender far more than restoring our bodies. While that may happen, God will not waste sickness like a trite revenge. No. He will use it to mold our minds and our hearts to realize our fragile state and seek His face. Accepting our fragility is an act of surrendering to His power. And His power is always a gift.

Job says in chapter 9 verses 32-33, *"For he is not a man like me that I can answer him, that we can take each other to court. This is no mediator between us."*

Surrendering to God's power is also to surrender to His sovereignty.

This goes back to our previous discussions on control. Do we still eagerly pray for healing? Absolutely! Do we still search our hearts for sin and accept forgiveness? Yes! But God deserves our faith in Him, not just in healing.

In Daniel chapter 3, Shadrach, Meshach, and Abednego put it plainly when they told the king *"But even if He does not rescue us,[g] we want you as king to know that we will not serve your gods or worship the gold statue you set up."*

Do you think like that? *But even if He does not*...end our suffering, pain, heal us etc.

The "but" is powerful here. Some versions say the word "and". This is pointing to the fact that God is God and He can. But (or and) if He doesn't, we know He is still God and sovereign and good and just and His ways are higher than ours. Even if we confess our sins, our righteousness acts are like rags compared to His glory and goodness...even in our sickness.

In chapter 13 Job says, *"You put my feet in the stocks and stand watch over my paths, setting a limit for the soles of my feet."*. How marvelous that we can completely trust the God we serve to watch over our unknown paths even when He limits us from walking on them yet! Even when we are sick and stopped from doing anything about it, He is not halted! He is at work for our benefit! Our surrendered dependence on Him is not a loss! It is a gain!

Whether he heals or slays us, Job reminds that our Redeemer lives (chapter 19:25)! He is the Redeemer of all things. Our minds, our souls, and our bodies. He determines when and how that happens, but we can be at rest knowing that it will.

Job had some ignorant friends, but I do believe in giving credit when credit is due. In chapter 37:14, Elihu tells Job to stop and consider *God's wonders*.

Oh, I believe God used this exact moment as the turning point in Job's surrender! Sometimes even a donkey speaks wise words!

It was not many verses later that the Lord's reply to all of Job's questioning and complaining finally comes forth. And came forth it did! It was this moment when the Lord helped Job get a grand perspective by naming God's wonders in such glorious beauty that Job's understanding of God's personal interest in all of His creation, including him, changed everything!

Read Chapter 38-39

What wonders stuck out to you as the most *powerful*?

_____
_____
_____
_____
_____
_____

What wonders stuck out to you as the most *personal*?

_____
_____
_____
_____
_____
_____

Read Chapter 40:1-5

Describe Job's reply in your own words.

_____
_____
_____
_____
_____
_____

Is this inspiring or what? By Job turning his focus to the Almighty and His personal and powerful wonders, Job's reasons to complain and question didn't go away, but they no longer had power over him in the light of God the Creator. God wasn't shoving His glory in Job's face. He was reordering Job's perspective which yielded a supernatural surrender of even Job's words. When we are in awe of God, there is no room for demanding anything else.

And for good measure, God continues His majesty through the next 2 chapters, but first He prepares Job that He is going to eventually require a response when He is finished and gives Job time to be able to adjust and choose his words carefully.

Read Chapter 42:1-6. Is there any indication that Job's pain, grief, or sickness changed? _____

I don't think so either. But something did change.

How do you view Job's heart in these verses? How is it different?
_____
_____
_____

God restored what was taken from Job in unquestionably personal ways. While it is never mentioned whether Job was healed of his diseased body, he lived for 140 years, which to me indicates a healthy enough existence to father many more children and thrive.

In the beginning of this book, I mentioned that you don't have to relate to my story. You don't have to relate to Job's either. Our outcomes and unique moments are truly a love story between God and his individual creation. You don't have to be physically sick to need healing. e all need healing. Sanctification is a gradual healing of the human condition. Time and time again what we will continue to see together is that, regardless of the details and the result of each story, the repeated connection that binds us all is God's pursuit of our personal surrender.

CHAPTER 3
Loss to Surrender

God is the ultimate caretaker of anything or anyone we will ever love.

The Lord tends to deal with me in seemingly strange, but personal ways. When I study the Bible, I'm always amazed by the new connections the Holy Spirit makes in my mind. There are always the obvious "felt board" story lessons that we begin with when learning in Sunday school or reading a children's Bible. Those are so vital when we are young; they give us a general grasp of the importance of the Bible and its contents. As I have grown older, I continue to find more subtle and deeper meanings like a bottomless well of water to my ever-learning soul. This is exactly what happened when I began studying 1 Samuel and the story of Hannah, Samuel's mother.

Through God's providence, my husband and I did have children. I absolutely call it miraculous. First, a boy and then, two years later, a girl. Such fullness in these unexpected blessings. I cannot explain how it happened against all of the doctors' evidence that it wasn't possible. Certainly, there was medical proof of my body's limitations. Only God knows, in His infinite and intricate knowledge of the creation of life, how to circumvent that. I rejoiced in these gifts and I knew that was what they were. There was a humility that ran through my bones during this time. I was holding a perfectly timed-out life in my arms, not once, but twice. At no point did I look at my children's faces and think they should have come sooner or even easier. It's incredible how my dark days of longing vanished in the light of providence. This was a major turning point in my relationship with God, which is exactly what had been developing over the last few years. Recognizing my limits and my humanness in comparison to His Lordship over my life had begun an awkward, but forward-moving surrender.

Please read 1 Samuel chapter 1.

In chapter 1, Hannah finds herself in a tormented place. Her husband's other wife not only had been the one blessed with children, but Hannah was also mocked and made to feel of less worth because of her lack. We all know that her inability to conceive was just that. Inability. In connection with the previous chapter in this book, we know we are not able to heal our bodies and have very little control over them. Hannah couldn't fix her barrenness and she suffered. She knew that if she were to ever have a child, it would be completely up to God.

Her actions displayed this knowledge because she went to the temple and prayed directly to God. In those days, most people went through a priest to present their requests to God. The local priest, a man named Eli, even questioned if she were drunk since he saw her mouth moving from a distance as she asked the Lord to notice her affliction. Poor woman! She could not even pray in public without ridicule!

What I want to focus on is not the fact that God indeed did give her the blessing of a son, which, as I have humbly experienced, is a glorious miracle. Instead, I'd like to focus on one very special verse for now.

1 Samuel 1:11 says, *"Making a vow, she pleaded, "Lord of Hosts, if You will take notice of Your servant's affliction, remember and not forget me, and give Your servant a son,[a] I will give him to the*

Lord all the days of his life, and his hair will never be cut."

Other than knowing that her womb was under the care of God Almighty, Hannah knew something else. She knew something incredibly difficult for most Christians to accept, but if we open our spiritual eyes to the eternal truth Hannah knew, we find something so freeing. Hannah had already accepted that any child she would ever be given would never actually be hers.

Motherhood is often innate. I think of terms like "momma bear". We mommas proudly wear such titles! We are protective and nurturing. We can yell at the refs from the stands or drink two glasses of wine and hit send on a snippy email to a teacher, and maybe, just maybe, our helicopter parenting might be considered a little smothering at times. We love our kids. We want the best for our kids. We guide them and know them well. Whatever we do, extreme or not, we feel we are doing what is right for our kids.

Ours.

I can't imagine the incredible courage and selflessness it takes to let go of a child to be adopted. And yet, that is what God has done over and over. Our children are not ours to keep. In some ways, we are temporary, adoptive, earthly parents in the place of their Heavenly Father. Hannah already lived this truth well before her labor pains were ever felt.

I don't know why we often hear stories about people struggling to get pregnant and then at some point, when they cease trying, it happens. I know this isn't everyone. Not even close, but we do hear those stories, and it makes us wonder. About 4 years after my daughter was born, I wasn't feeling quite right, and because my hormone imbalances caused on-going problems, I went to my doctor. When the nurse came into the room and told me I was pregnant, nothing could have been more shocking. We had not tried again using medications or any procedures. It just "happened". I could not have been more overcome.

After several ultrasounds over a few months, it was discovered at 20 weeks that I was wrong. I could indeed be more shocked. Twins! Twin girls to be exact. If it's possible to be thrilled and terrified, then that was me. What an unexpected blessing, and what a rollercoaster coming our way! I had no idea how true that was.

Our joy was apparent, but so was an unexplained quiet from the ultrasound tech just moments after the news. When the doctor came in, he showed us that they could not see a membrane separating the twins, meaning they were in the same embryonic sack. This was not a normal development, and without us really understanding the severity of the situation, they scooted me next door for a 3D ultrasound at the high-risk pregnancy center.

Oh, to get a deep look at those two beautiful, small faces. Their hands were wrapped around each other, and their little bodies were lovingly intertwined. My heart was full of surprise and elation.

The familiar ominous feeling crowded the room when the doctor began to explain that the very sweetness of the twins intertwining bodies was the exact issue they feared. We learned that monoamniotic twins, though very rare, have a very high mortality rate due to the probable and eventual cut-off of blood supply and lack of oxygen because of their closeness. At 26 weeks I would need to be admitted to the hospital for 24-hour fetal heartbeat monitoring. In layman's terms, this pretty much meant that we would be waiting until we lost heartbeat detection and would need to rush an emergency c-section in hopes to get at least one baby out alive. Devastatingly, at 27 weeks, that is what happened.

Isla Quinn was born without a heartbeat. She was kept alive on life-support until I was awake enough to hold her for the first and last time. I felt her tiny body gently fall as they let her take her last machine-forced breath. No one can prepare you for that lifelessness.

Isabel Quinn was in the NICU for 30 days until her little lungs just couldn't fight anymore. Her death on the heels of her sister's was nothing short of a stabbing, slicing pain.

Just a few months earlier, these unexpected lives suddenly appeared, generated a new hope, and now they were gone.

I find it nearly impossible to choose words that exactly or adequately express what a moment is like when your child transitions from life to death. For me, it was a muddled mixture of oppressing, assaulting emotions. The idea that I would have to lay my child down in her hospital cradle and walk away, never to see her again, is the cruelest realization I have ever endured. They were both beyond beautiful and full of potential. I could see it in the details of their turned up little noses and their big searching eyes, the finger grips, and the muffled cries beyond the ventilators. The surprise of their existence and the hope of their future melted away with nothing left to show. It is still haunting to think of the elevator ride down to the parking lot, while holding an empty infant car seat.

I don't mean to strum your emotions for the sake of anything more than to set the stage for the beauty that would come from these ashes. I mentioned a few pages ago that Hannah knew the child she was praying for would never be hers. Even while she was painfully praying for the blessing of a son and the release of the torment of longing and social stain that she was experiencing, she vowed to give back her son to God.

I don't want us to miss what this means. Hannah knew that if God gave her a son, once the child was weaned, the boy would leave her arms and her home and permanently live in God's house. This means no bedtime stories, no daily hugs and kisses. She'd miss out on the childhood milestones and thousands of mother-son moments that any mother would grip onto with both fists rather than miss one.

Why then did Hannah let go of her son before he was even a reality? Knowing the longing she felt for him makes it hard to grasp her ability to do this! How?

I believe there are two reasons. The first is because she already knew he didn't belong to her and that God was the ultimate parent for her child. She also knew that although God places a desire to mother children, He also places within us a fulfilling purpose to worship Him above all things. These truths brought her great comfort. So, she surrendered her rights to the little one she prayed for to the great ONE to whom she knew he belonged.

Hannah gave her only son to the Lord because she knew her eternal purpose trumped her earthly purposes by a landslide. In verses 3-8 of 1 Samuel chapter 1 it says,

"3 Year after year this man went up from his town to worship and sacrifice to the Lord Almighty at Shiloh, where Hophni and Phinehas, the two sons of Eli, were priests of the Lord. 4 Whenever the day came for Elkanah to sacrifice, he would give portions of the meat to his wife Peninnah and to all her sons and daughters. 5 But to Hannah he gave a double portion because he loved her, and the Lord had closed her womb. 6 Because the Lord had closed Hannah's womb, her rival kept provoking her in order to irritate her. 7 This went on year after year. Whenever Hannah went up to the house of the Lord, her rival provoked her till she wept and would not eat. 8 Her husband Elkanah would say to her, "Hannah, why are you weeping? Why don't you eat? Why are you downhearted? Don't I mean more to you than ten sons?"

Did you catch that? Hannah had a husband who absolutely adored her, despite her not bearing him children. Elkanah, Hannah's husband, was truly a rare man in those days. To be valued and treasured by him just for being herself and not for what she could give him was something any husbandless woman would dream of. I don't think Hannah was unappreciative, but in those days as a wife but not a mother, Hannah was only fulfilling half of her earthly purpose. So, if Hannah wanted more than a loving husband, more than to stop the ridicule, and desired so deeply for God to open her womb, why did she give Samuel away?

Hannah knew by proof of her actions that her purpose was not in her loving husband, nor the bearing of children. Her purpose was not so temporary and fleeting. Her purpose was beyond the satisfaction of human fulfillment. Her purpose and her treasures were residing in her heart all along. Her purpose would be fulfilled THROUGH her son, not IN her son!

Her purpose was eternal; to further God's Kingdom through her own sacrifice and surrender.

How does this change our perspective? Whether your loss is a child, or another dear loved one, you are faced with letting go of your rights to them. The moment our second twin's chest stopped seeking breath, there was a split second of relief that fell over me in the midst of my angst. Safe. My girls are safe in His arms. Together. As they were meant to be. My job as a mother to protect them and teach them God's ways was no longer needed. They made it right back into their Creator's arms where we will all be someday. Any joy that I would take in experiencing this short life here with them is nothing compared to the joy that my Father in Heaven is experiencing with them now. Surrendering my natural motherly desires to their eternal pleasure in His presence was a deeply painful, but also very freeing, and strangely, a satisfying sacrifice. This truth doesn't erase my longing and the grief I experienced. Instead it was coupled with it. Their eternal Father's love for them kept my grief from overtaking me and gently and lovingly pushed my focus on Him rather than them.

My purpose is not in my children; though I revel in them. I fight my own grip on their lives and I tried to seer their little faces in my memory when they were young. But when I faced never seeing my twins' faces again, I had no option but to ask myself what my eternal purpose is. It isn't them. They are bonus! A massive gift I am never going to be worthy of borrowing. No. Instead, I am His. He is why I live and get to love anyone He loves.

Hannah was a wise woman. But she was a woman, a human. Just because her story turned out well, doesn't mean surrendering her loss of her rights to her son was anything short of naturally difficult; maybe even heart-breaking. Surrendering is never easy, at least at first. But it is also never without blessing in the end. Her sacrifice was used, through her son Samuel, to bring about King David's reign and eventually ushered in the Savior of the world, Jesus Christ.

Read 1 Samuel 1:21-28

Hannah not only vowed to give her son to the Lord if the Lord granted her prayer, she followed through with a heart of surrender.

What was the last word in verse 21?
_____

In addition to taking young Samuel to Eli, what else did she bring with her in verse 24?
_____

Hannah demonstrated surrender through sacrifice. She was literally giving away her first-born son, whom she desperately prayed for for years, but she didn't do this with a begrudging heart. As a matter of fact, her husband just a few verses before told her "Do what you think is best."

Against anything we have to offer our loved ones, isn't them being in His presence the BEST? There is nothing better. While we sacrifice our desires to be with those we love so dearly, loving them through sacrificing our rights to hang on is the ultimate act of surrender. We trust God and can even rejoice in the gift of those we love being eternally with Him.

Read 1 Samuel 2:1-10

Hannah had just surrendered her son to the Lord's service. What were her first words?

_____

Imagine yourself in her shoes. What are some statements that Hannah makes that impact you?

_____
_____
_____
_____
_____
_____

We don't often feel like surrendering when it comes to loss, but God can help us focus on His goodness. Describe your great loss. Do you trust God with this loss? What do you need Him to help you with concerning your loss? Write your heartfelt prayer to Him here.

_____
_____
_____
_____
_____
_____
_____
_____

CHAPTER 4
Injury to surrender

Our injury is not our banner. Our redemption is.

When our twins passed, my husband and I found it very difficult to continue day to day life. One of the NICU doctors pulled us aside before we left the hospital and gently told us that the percentage of divorce is very high in families who experience the death of a child, let alone two. Admittedly, the weight of the statement created a slight alarm, but at the time I could barely manage my grieving emotions. There wasn't room to entertain this thought too.

Though the entire situation was horrendous, I am grateful for the doctors and nurses who cared so deeply for us and our babies. I remember a nurse telling me that grief was like waves in the ocean. They may hit you out of nowhere, but little by little they bring you to shore. I found this to be terribly true. I could be walking along in the cereal aisle with my other 2 young children and a smack of breath-stealing pain would stop me in my tracks. As far as the "bringing me to shore" part, I had a long way to go.

We all handle grief in different ways. In the coming months I noticed that my husband and I handled it very differently and in different time frames. It was incredibly hard to relate to one another. There was an uncomfortable estrangement that grew, and anytime we tried to force connection, it seemed to build resentment. I didn't want to call it that, but that is what it was.

I should be clear here for a minute.

The death of our twins was not the catalyst of our marriage troubles; it revealed those troubles. Tragedy tends to sift us. It shakes out all of the distractions and rudely points to our weaknesses and strengths. Sometimes in relationships this is when we find out how vast they are. Satan would like nothing more than to dig a canyon between those differences so we don't recognize the bridge that God can be between them.

Though spirituality was never contentious between us, it was never bonding either. In many ways, my husband and I lived different lives. I can look back now and say that neither of us wanted it to be that way, but we didn't know how to fix it, and we probably didn't think that was possible. When you don't think there is an answer, sometimes you don't seek it. You just keep going on until you can't anymore, and that is what we were facing.

In the years before, it was painfully revealed that my husband had some addictive behaviors. I was deeply hurt and worried but with no tools in my toolbelt and little confidence for positive change, I was at a loss apart from God's intervention. Going back to the idea that people might not seek answers when they feel there isn't one, I had naively hoped and passively prayed for a change and pressed on. I got really good at ignoring them; afraid to rock the sinking boat.

On December 4, 2010, just 4 months after the loss of our twins, I woke up violently remembering a horrible dream. I began to tell my husband of the details. I had been lost in a large city, going from rooftop to rooftop trying to find him. I struggled with elevators not working and taxi cabs passing me by. Each rooftop was empty until I got to the one on the tallest building in the city. A long table, covered in white cloth, was surrounded by people dressed up in suits and formal attire. At the end of the table was a woman in a wedding dress and an opaque veil covering her face. My husband was standing on the left side of her, lifting her veil to reveal her lovely face and her long dark curls. It wasn't me. She was the complete opposite of me in every way. I screamed at him trying to get his attention, but audible words escaped me. The dream ended there.

My husband had listened to my tale silently. When it was done, he got up from the bed and went into the kitchen. I was a little hurt, but I headed to the bathroom needing a hot shower. My head was foggy. Our distance and our silence were so loud. Not a minute later, my life took a very sharply angled turn. He entered the bathroom and without hesitation, began to tell me he was having an affair. His face was sullen and trapped-looking.

I threw out questions and cringed at the answers. I do not want to focus on salacious details here nor take any time to heap blame upon him. There is no benefit for anyone in doing so. What I knew at that moment was that the veil had indeed come off. My veil. There was no longer the luxury of ducking my head and plugging away as usual. No more ignoring. Whatever glaze was still on my eyes wasted away. I was staring at pain behind me, pain in the present, and more pain to come. I felt surrounded and choked.

Betrayal is a deep, infectious wound. It causes injury unlike any loss or grief. It's a wound that has the great potential to re-open over and over again. It nearly seems impossible for it to heal by the hands of another human. Even if my husband had brokenly repented for this injury, fear and doubt would have battled for residence within my wound. But, repentance didn't happen. Begging forgiveness didn't occur. There was a cold emptiness in his eyes. He felt very justified, and my wound festered.

In the next chapter, I will explain more, but I would like to help us make some important and intentional connections with the Bible here.

Emotional injury is always a result of betrayal. We feel injured because someone whom we trusted decided to choose someone or something over us. Maybe they are justified, but it doesn't lessen the hurt. It doesn't have to be a marital situation.

Anytime a person believed there was an agreement between them and someone else and it was broken, the result is a feeling of betrayal. This might even be one-sided. One party might feel there is an agreement, and the other, not so much.

Certainly, you have experienced a feeling of betrayal of some sort. Or, maybe you were the one who caused injury to someone else. We can get mighty pious when experiencing an injurious betrayal.

As I mentioned, this doesn't just apply to marital injury. When a spouse commits betrayal, it's called adultery. But when a Christian betrays God, what is that called?

Take a look a Hosea 4:12 *"My people consult their wooden idols, and their divining rods inform them. For a spirit of promiscuity leads them astray; they act promiscuously in disobedience to their God."*

You don't have to have a wooden idol to relate. Betraying God through any sin is both adulterous *and* idolatrous. We are a sinful people, and anything we choose above and beyond choosing God is adulterous and idolatrous. We hear the word "sin" a lot. I doubt we go through a church service without hearing it at least once. It is the word we use to state that we cheated on God. We cheated on the covenant He made with us.

I had often wondered why God, in all of His omniscience, would make a covenant in the first place if He knew we would break it. Would I have stood at the altar and accepted a vow from my husband if I knew he was going to break it? Of course not! But why then did God? Why even have a covenant that would never last? I want you to imagine God standing with you in a church that is covered in wedding decorations and surrounded by smiling friends and family. He is looking at you with kind and loving eyes, as though you are the most incredible thing that He's ever known. You can see He feels proud that YOU are His. But, you are standing there knowing for certain that you do not plan to keep your faithfulness vow to Him. Maybe you want to, but you know your evil desires all too well. You hide your temptations and you have no doubt that repeatedly you will cause pain to the One forsaking all others and choosing you. Yet, you say nothing. Before the officiant speaks a ceremonious word, your Heavenly Groom leans forward and whispers softly so that only you can hear, "It's ok, my love, I know... I choose you anyway."

The imagery here is an example of the real covenant God made with us. He already knew we would not want to nor be able to adhere to our covenant. He chose us anyway, over and over! The gift He was getting in us was worth the injury He already knew He would sustain. The covenant was not for Him in the first place. God does not sin nor break His promises. He doesn't need anything signed on paper to prove His word.

The covenant was for us.

He knew we needed a covenant to reveal two things to us. The first revelation is that God keeps His promises to us. We needed a promise --a covenant -- to see through our own doubt that He always keeps His word. Whether we doubt or not, He is faithful and adores us. He fights for us and stays present. His eyes do not wander. As a matter of fact, He doesn't even sleep. He is with us always and is everything we ever need. His covenant offers an enormously unfair amount of one-sided benefits to us that we could never offer Him in return. The covenant was to make us eternally secure regardless of our own affairs.

For example, God told Hosea in chapter 1 to go and marry a woman who already had a promiscuous reputation. God knew, and Hosea knew, that just because a marriage covenant would be agreed upon between them, it would not mean that, all of a sudden, this woman would turn over a new leaf and become a crocheting, coupon-cutting, faithfully loving wife. Just the opposite. God was creating a staged scene for Israel to see what His own relationship with them was like. God chose them as His bride while fully aware of their inability to keep their covenant. His desire and ability to keep His part continued. Hosea did the same. He kept his faithful promise to his unfaithful wife, Gomer, regardless of her actions. This was a tangible and an *agape* example of an intangible one-sided, faithful relationship.

The initial covenant offers us a second revelation; our incapability to keep it because we are sinful. I am going to go into this further in the next chapter, but we actually need to have a standard to be held to in order to know we have failed. If there was not a standard, we wouldn't know if we succeeded or failed. If we do not think we have failed, then we do not know we have injured the One with whom we are in a covenant! In a marriage, we promise to be faithful. That is the standard. If the standard wasn't there, then we wouldn't know if we have injured the other person. Our sin is our adulterous broke standard against our covenant and our God.

I think that so often we don't choose to consider the person we are injuring when we are sinning. We are choosing to satisfy our sinful desires, and that becomes our focus. We ignore the standard and break the covenant through our justification. We needed a covenant with God to face our sin and the grief it caused our ever-faithful Groom. Without someone we might injure, we could go on sinning and justifying all we want!

The Bible's continued use of the model of the marriage covenant demonstrates how God continued to accept His people's repentance through their sacrifices, yet they continued to break their vows and sin against His laws.

Have you heard about couples who have gotten divorced and remarried again? It's rare, but there is something really special about that. A second covenant. God chose to form a second covenant with us, but even in a second covenant He knew we couldn't keep it. He Himself had not made a mistake the first time, and He wasn't making a second mistake either. As stated before, we needed the first one to see that we could not remain faithful. So, what about the second?

The second covenant was not like the first. While the standard of faithfulness still exists, and our inability to measure up continued, the means to achieve faithfulness completely changed. No more sacrificial doves or rituals. Nothing we could do would ever enable us to keep His laws or His standards, nor could we match His faithfulness. So, God did something incredible! This is where Jesus enters stage right.

> Jeremiah 31:31-34 *"Behold, the days are coming, declares the Lord, when I will make a new covenant with the house of Israel and the house of Judah, not like the covenant that I made with their fathers on the day when I took them by the hand to bring them out of the land of Egypt, my covenant that they broke, though I was their husband, declares the Lord. But this is the covenant that I will make with the house of Israel after those days, declares the Lord: I will put my law within them, and I will write it on their hearts. And I will be their God, and they shall be my people. And no longer shall each one teach his neighbor and each his brother, saying, 'Know the Lord,' for they shall all know me, from the least of them to the greatest, declares the Lord. For I will forgive their iniquity, and I will remember their sin no more."*

> Jeremiah 23:5 *"Behold, the days are coming,"* declares the Lord, *"When I will raise up from David a righteous [c]Branch."*

Jeremiah was an anointed prophet, and this spoken word was hundreds of years before God established a new, second covenant with His people. God doesn't take so long because He needs the time. Instead, He knows *we* need the time to recognize that we need Him! He sets the stage for us to accept our own failures and readies our hearts for His great, undeserving, and sacrificial love.

Imagine that wedding ceremony again exactly as before. God still whispers that he knows you will not be faithful, and he chooses you anyway. Typically, unfaithfulness may be grounds for divorce. But, God wants a relationship with you so desperately, that He already has a plan to *prevent* divorce in the event of your inevitable unfaithfulness. The thought of being separated from you is too much for Him to bear. So, He turns to His son sitting in the front row and calls Him up to the front and pulls out a scroll of paper. A divorce decree. The decree has a lengthy list of every sin you ever have and will ever commit against Him. Every betrayal. Every evil thought. All of it listed there in terrible detail.

Right there is every justifiable reason He has to turn away and leave you at the altar. But, instead, He gives the pen to His son to sign the divorce decree as the new owner of your betrayal. The name it bears is Jesus. Instead of divorcing you, He divorces His own Son.

This, sweet friend, is our new covenant through God's Son taking our place. A forever acknowledgement that we cannot stay faithful to a faithful God and that He chooses us anyway to bestow His love upon us and for us to spend an underserved eternity with Him.

We don't get to hang onto injury like a justly waving banner. Yes, you have been injured. Maybe in terrible and dark ways. Clearly, so have I. Yes, the pain is real and may last a long time. You will have healing to go through, and God desires to be with you the whole way, directing that healing. You may never receive "closure" or even an apology. But, it is vital to our Christian growth to understand that we do not have the right to continue being a victim. We may still hurt, and we may be a victim, but we don't have to stay as one. We are set free in Christ and we must surrender that right to be jailed in injury. We don't see Christ holding tightly to the wounds we have inflicted on Him like a badge of pride or means to gain justification for His feelings. Instead, He surrendered His rights to them in the Garden of Gethsemane in order to love us fully.

At first, the thought of surrendering our injuries to God

sways us to think this means we are giving the inflictor a "get out of jail free" pass. Remember this: when someone sins against another, they are also sinning against God. He is their judge and jury. I am not saying you present yourself as a target to people who injured you. I am not saying that we continue allowing injury. Boundaries are good and healthy, and part of setting up boundaries is seeking healing so that God can use it for His glory.

Yet, it is not our right to seek revenge, force repentance or obedience, create more shame and guilt, or even to convict. God is not only your God. He is your betrayer's God too, and only He knows how to also uniquely pursue their heart through the masterful and strategic voice of the Holy Spirit. Even if we could bring these things about, He would do it better. Only He is the healer and absolver of sin. As the injured party, we must surrender the temptation to fix or change those who hurt us. Can we say "Ouch" and "Stop"? Absolutely. But we must surrender the idea that it's our job to help the injuring party see clearly or force them to rectify the wrong. Jesus told the crowd in Matthew 5:44 to love and pray for their enemies. He doesn't tell us to debate and berate. Or whine and shame. Nor continue being the victim. No. Love and pray. And sometimes that can be from afar.

If in this life you get to see the rare instance of earthly justice occur when a wrong is done, it is not unusual to experience a lack of satisfaction. The wrong was still committed. People still got hurt. There is no undoing it. Only Jesus' sacrifice truly sets us free. When we realize the unfair torture He chose to endure on behalf of our wrongs, it's difficult to hang on to our own injury. Instead of focusing on the pain, we surrender it to Him. He sees your injury. He has unending compassion and hurts when you hurt. He is the righter of wrongs and we can be free to surrender the spinning of our wheels to make those wrongs right.

Read about God's first covenant with His people below.

Exodus 19:3-8 Then Moses went up to God, and the Lord called to him from the mountain and said, "This is what you are to say to the descendants of Jacob and what you are to tell the people of Israel: 4 'You yourselves have seen what I did to Egypt, and how I carried you on eagles' wings and brought you to myself. 5 Now if you obey me fully and keep my covenant, then out of all nations you will be my treasured possession. Although the whole earth is mine, 6 you[a] will be for me a kingdom of priests and a holy nation.' These are the words you are to speak to the Israelites." ⁷ So Moses went back and summoned the elders of the people and set before them all the words the Lord had commanded him to speak. ⁸ The people all responded together, "We will do everything the Lord has said." So Moses brought their answer back to the Lord.

In verse 5 God says to obey Him _____ and keep His _____.

In verses 7-8, how did the people respond to His request? _____

God knew that, even if their response was genuine at the time, they simply would never be able to keep their promise.

Read Hosea 1:1-2 What word goes in the blank?

"…for the land is committing _____ of promiscuity by abandoning the Lord."

In Hosea 3: 3 Hosea tells Gomer his wife to come and live with him, but she is not to be promiscuous or belong to any other man and then what does he promise her?

In what ways do you feel betrayed? How did that betrayal injure you?
_____
_____
_____

Forgiveness is another form of surrendering our right to be injured.

Read Colossians 3:12-13. What does it call us to "put on"?

_____

After you reread the last sentence, explain why.
_____
_____

We are all betrayers of some sort. In what ways do you need to ask for forgiveness for your betrayal and injury toward God and others?

_____
_____
_____

CHAPTER 5
Sin to Surrender

Even truth that hurts is still a swift vessel to   freedom

I absolutely love rollercoasters! Always have. I remember going to an amusement park called Boardwalk and Baseball when I was in marching band and playing in a competition there. It was the first time I took on an upside-down coaster. I couldn't get enough. As soon as the ride ended, my buddies and I ran straight to the ride entrance and got on again. Not long ago I took my own kids to a thrill ride park and jumped on the fastest coaster they had, but it didn't go quite the same way it had when I was young. Was that nausea with a dash of dizziness? My kids wanted to get right back on, but I needed to sit down for a minute. Later, I learned that the inner ear thickens when you age and that sometimes this and other changes cause some equilibrium sensitivity. I was annoyed that I felt like this. I loved these rides! Yet, I hated feeling nauseous, and my days of repeated rollercoaster riding were now slowing. I prefer to keep my equilibrium intact.

Nausea can stop you in your tracks. It strips away whatever you had planned for the day. It takes over and makes it hard to imagine feeling better, but, at some point, you do. When you are deeply injured by someone else's sin, it is very difficult to believe that you will ever not feel injured again. It is sickening. The pain of the injury takes over our senses. It is difficult to think. It slows everything down. Yet, processing what has happened is a must.

Sometimes we rerun the happenings over and over. Sometimes we try to push it away because it is so terrible to think about. Regardless of which way the brain deals with it, it is trauma. Trauma is not just emotional. It affects the whole body and affects different people differently. I learned during the time of my deepest injury that I tend to freeze. Some fight, some take flight. I freeze.

I couldn't stop replaying everything. I would lay in bed unable to move forward. My husband was not truly interested in fixing our marriage. He came home for a year, slightly attempted counseling, but for the most part he was just there. Not present. This lack of enthusiasm deepened the injury. I was frozen and drowning.

It's interesting how you think you know what you would do in a situation until you are actually in it. I never imagined that I would, or could, entertain the thought of trying to save a marriage after adultery, but I did want to, desperately. I loved him and our family, as dysfunctional as it was. Unfortunately, it takes two, and after about a year, the second person in our marriage determined that he wanted a divorce. He was so far away in so many ways at this point. Only God could reach him. Not me.

The divorce paperwork was filed, but I couldn't shake something a pastor at our church said to me many months before. We had asked for a meeting with him to talk about our circumstance and I naively hoped to get some quick fixes. That, of course, didn't happen. At some point during the conversation the pastor interrupted our talk and asked my husband to wait outside the office. I was a little taken back by this. Frankly, it seemed the opposite of what I would have expected. Why was it not my husband sitting here for a one-on-one shake down? Shouldn't he be the person sweating nervously in this chair?

When the door closed, the pastor's face got quite serious. He leaned forward and, in paraphrase, said, "Megan, I believe that what you know and what you see about your husband's failures in this marriage is only the tip of the iceberg. I have counseled many people in your shoes, and I feel strongly that the deception in your marriage is deep and wide, if you are going to choose to try to continue, you need to know two things. First, no matter what is beneath this ocean, no matter how dark and dirty your husband's sin is, yours is just as dark and dirty in the eyes of God. Without the saving blood of Christ, you are just as filthy and unworthy. You are equal. You are equal in both sin and in new life and, until you can see yourself and your husband this way, the chances of your marriage being saved, let alone being healthy, is very low. Secondly, it is true that God hates divorce. It's also true that by the Bible's standard's you have every right to divorce your husband because of his affair. God is a God of restoration, and it would be for His glory should your marriage survive and thrive through this terrible wound. Ultimately, you are free from sin in this choice. However, there is something that is far more important to God than the restoration of your marriage: the restoration of your husband's relationship with his Savior. God can reach your husband either way, but in the quiet of your heart, what will you desire and pray for *more* during this time? His spirit's restoration or your marriage restoration? If you can fully accept all of this, then you will experience healing, peace, and intimacy with your Savior unlike anything you've ever known, regardless of the result of your marriage."

I was stunned.

This wasn't exactly the couple's pastoral counseling I was expecting. No finger shaking to my adulterous husband bringing about repentance. No pat on my back and a list of how my husband was going to fix this.

What I did get was something far more valuable. Freedom. This may surprise you. It wasn't wrapped in a sweet package of padded words. It was surrounded by seemingly ugly truth that was ultimately the medicine I needed more than anything else to bring healing to my soul. Yes. My husband was guilty, and we were all suffering. I wanted my heart to be fixed. I wanted my husband to be "fixed". However, what I needed more than anything was freedom.

You see, during this year of trying to save my marriage, I spent a shameful amount of time trying to "help" my husband see his sinful ways. This was not intentionally with a haughty or prideful heart. I genuinely wanted to see change in him; for him to experience the joy of our salvation. Peace. Healing. Beauty from our ashes. I wanted the big marriage miracle. But in doing so, it created a thicker wedge between us. I pushed, and he pulled away. People don't reach surrender for, or because of, other people. God is the heart changer. Not me. It's not my job to reach my husband, and the Lord was freeing me of that as long as I was willing to surrender it.

I also began to see hope that my pastor's words were true. I began to search my soul for my own sin. Here is a fair warning. If you choose to turn your attention from someone else's sin to your own, do not be surprised when the floodgates open. There was one day I spent on the bathroom floor both praying and receiving forgiveness for I do not know how long. Hours I am sure. I had not been an award-winning wife. I was able to start to see the areas I had failed, apart from my injury. My failure didn't justify the adultery, but God used it as another means of getting my attention. I had much to surrender. Worship flowed out of me like a broken dam. My eyes were open to my wretchedness. There was a humility that began to grow. Not a human form of humbleness. I have never been a proud person, but a new open-handed surrender began. This was different. This was deeper. It was beautiful. When I surrendered my sin to Jesus, He filled the void in my heart with hope. Not simply a hope for healing in my marriage. Hope in Him and that, whatever came next, He loved me and I was not alone. I knew the confidence in Him that grew out of my humility was lasting.

1 John 4, beginning in verse 7, speaks of perfect love. It has become my life chapter because very early on in my Christian

walk, I admitted to myself that I did not love God. I wanted to, but I didn't know how. The only way to reciprocate God's love is by receiving it. Until these first two steps happened, I would be incapable of loving my husband through this mess we were in. I had begun studying 1 John 4 during this time, and this living Word showed me that the foundation of God's love for me is 100% undeserved sacrifice. He owes me nothing, and I get everything. I owe Him everything, and I can give Him nothing other than accepting His everything! Without His Son's sacrifice, my sin is on equal ground with not only my husband's, but with any and every evil sin in the history of man. Yet, now, the perfect Savior's blood makes me equal to Him and His righteousness. That is what love is. God sees me as He sees His Son. This is how I must learn to look at and love my husband.

What my pastor knew was that I could not reach this sacrificial love without looking square in the face of my own sin and realizing God's capability to love me anyway. Now, I get it.

. 1 John 4:20-21 says *"If anyone says, "I love God," yet hates his brother, he is a liar. For the person who does not love his brother he has seen cannot love the God he has not seen.[j]21 And we have this command from Him: The one who loves God must also love his brother.*

I could use up the rest of these pages listing the sin I faced. Willful and unwillful sin. But, I won't do that. What I can say is that I was not innocent in the struggles of our marriage. Sometimes my fault was ignorance, but certainly not innocent. Yet, God loved me. I can't give that kind of sacrificial and undeserved love on my own. He made it possible to love my husband through my own rejection because I was accepted in Christ. It opened up the way for me to desire my husband's restoration and personal healing more than the healing of my marriage. I surrendered the silent kicking and screaming tantrums that I was owed, once I realized I am owed nothing. The Lord shifted those tantrums to a prayerful desire for my husband to someday know and surrender to that perfect love 1 John speaks of.

When we face our sin, whether on our own or when confronted, we often experience sorrow. There are two kinds of sorrow mentioned in the Bible concerning God's people facing their own sin; Godly sorrow and worldly sorrow. Only one leads to true surrender.

David was an incredible man in the Bible. He had it all. 1 Samuel 16:18 says, one of the servants answered, *"I have seen a son of Jesse of Bethlehem who knows how to play the lyre. He is a brave man and a warrior. He speaks well and is a fine-looking man. And the Lord is with him."*

The man was talented, good looking, eloquent, and, best of all, the Lord was with him. I'm thinking this guy wouldn't have lasted long on a dating app. The list continues as we see the Bible play out his accomplishments done in the name of the Lord. From battles fought and won, cities taken, kingship granted, psalms written and sung to bless the ages, multiple wives and children continuing his line all the way to Jesus, the list goes on. Yet, David was human. Even David, in all of his "man after God's own heart" ways, was an equal to the rest of us. Isaiah 54:6 tells us: *"All of us have become like something unclean, and all our righteous acts are like a polluted garment; all of us wither like a leaf, and our iniquities carry us away like the wind."*

Even David wasn't worthy of God's sacrificial love, and he knew it. He was a humble man. The Psalms are full of his humility, even when rebuked. If you remember in 2 Samuel 11 and 12, David lusted after Bathsheba, got her pregnant, and when his plans failed to cover it up, David set up Bathsheba's husband to be killed in battle. When Nathan approached David in chapter 12 with a parable about the rich man taking a poor man's sheep, David's reaction to the unfair treatment was righteous and just. He saw the cruelty and selfishness. When Nathan used this story to help David see that the selfish rich man was actually David himself, David waved the white flag. 2 Samuel 12:13 tells us that David simply said, "I have sinned against the Lord." No excuses. Just the surrendered truth. His sorrow was a Godly sorrow and led to surrender immediately. He received a terrible consequence through the death of his son and turned toward God.

Later, in 2 Samuel 24, David intentionally forced a census count that increased the total number of the population. Some say this was out of pride, but whatever the intention, he purposefully had the count skewed.

When reproached by the prophet Gad, David did not lay out a series of justifications. Instead, verse 10 states, *"David was conscience-stricken after he had counted the fighting men, and he said to the Lord, "I have sinned greatly in what I have done. Now, Lord, I beg you, take away the guilt of your servant. I have done a very foolish thing."*

The consequence for David's sin affected the nation. So often we forget that our sin does not just affect ourselves. There is always a ripple effect of some kind toward others which is all the more reason to reach humility when we sin. When David saw a plague fall upon his people, David's heart was grieved for his people and not just himself. This is another fruit of Godly sorrow. It shows a surrendering of self and empathy for how our sin affects others. He desired to sacrifice at the altar, and Araunah the Jebusite offered David to take animals on the threshing floor to sacrifice without paying, but David said, *"No, I insist on paying you for it. I will not sacrifice to the Lord my God burnt offerings that cost me nothing."* Godly sorrow costs us. At minimum, if we are repentant of our sins, it requires our surrender, and that is when the restoration begins.

Worldly sorrow, however, does not bear the fruit of surrender. Read 1 Samuel 15 and answer the questions below.

In verse 3, what were God's specific instructions to Saul?

Did he follow those instructions in verse 8 and 9? _____

Read verse 12. What did Saul do that shows his heart and mind were only thinking of himself.

_____
_____

Saul was not a humble man. Even when he was reproached, humility was not evident. Verse 11 says that the Lord was grieved that he made Saul king. When a man sins and grieves the One who anointed him as king, yet is not humbled by his God's grief, only destruction is in his future.

When Samuel confronted the king in verse 14, who did Saul blame in verse 15?

_____

Write out verse 17 in our own words.

_____
_____

Until we see what God has done for us and how we deserved none of it, we react in worldly sorrow. But, when we face our sin and revel in His loving grace, we can't help but display Godly sorrow and surrender ourselves to Him. We then find joy in our salvation!

What does Samuel say will happen to Saul in verse 23?

_____
_____

Now that Saul was going to experience a consequence, he began to admit his sin, but this was not a result of humility. In verse 27 he ripped Samuel's robe out of frustration because he wasn't going to get his way. In verse 30 he asked Samuel to honor him before the elders and the people. Does this sound like a surrendered man?

Facing our own sin in the light of God's perfect love brings about surrender. We become so grateful for the gift of grace we have been given that we can't help ourselves but to ooze humility. It's very difficult to hold fault against another when you grasp what you have been so undeservedly given.

CHAPTER 6
Wrestling to Surrender

It is an honor and a privilege to wrestle with the God of the stars.

My hope is that what you have read so far has shown how personally and intentionally God uses anything we face, both good and difficult, to lead us toward surrendering to Him by trusting He is good. Surrendering is always rewarded with more of Him. He is truly our personal Savior, and the more we move into surrender, the more we understand how intimate of a Savior He is.

There are many forms of intimacy. Certainly, we understand the connections of physical intimacy, but let's branch out a bit. What are the requirements of intimacy? Do you have to know someone for years to feel intimately connected to them? Do you have to have a label like spouse, friend, daughter etc.? Does intimacy occur only in pleasant and positive circumstances? I'm sure you have some answers of your own to these questions, and I'll bet that they are drawn from your experiences.

Intimacy does come in many forms, but no matter how it occurs, it requires surrender of some kind. You can't hide and be intimate at the same time. You can't give into fear and be intimate. You can't be selfish and be intimate. Intimacy is a two-way street where both parties meet by choosing to be vulnerable and join in a mutually empathetic experience.

During my divorce and beyond I was insatiably hungry for truth. I feared my emotions leading me because they were all over the place. My shower became my unintentional prayer closet. I did not plan that. As a matter of fact, I escaped to the shower mostly because it was about the only place that I could find alone time, away from my two adorable young children constantly wanting my attention. I could clear my head and find focus in the white noise of the hot water. I could play back my thoughts on teachings and scripture I had heard throughout the week. I could pray better there in the steam, undistracted, and it seemed that the Holy Spirit's voice was even just a little crisper during these moments. I began to experience a sweetness, and I treasured this quiet time every day. To this day, that is my go-to place to hear Him the best. It is like we have created a secret room where we meet far away from the world.

But, these moments have not always felt sweet and pleasant. As a matter of fact, some of the most intimate moments I have experienced in my shower prayer closet (especially during my "divorce era") were quite painful.

Think about that cruel night when Jesus excruciatingly wept to His Father in the garden before His crucifixion. He was fully aware of the truth, yet He wept. The truth was that He was meant to be tortured and mocked and broken for us within a matter of hours, and He knew it. He knew the truth that His death would save us from ourselves. If anyone denies that you can experience both joy and anguish at the same time, I challenge them on this. Knowing the truth, and even agreeing with it, doesn't necessarily mean we won't wrestle with it. And that's what Jesus did. He painfully wept, and His body ached in anticipation of the gruesome day to come, so He spent an intimate and terrible night with His Father. Intimacy is beautiful even when it doesn't look beautiful. Jesus was wrestling with His human emotions against the eternal truth He believed in, lived for, and accepted.

I used to watch wrestling when I was a "tween". I think I liked the wildly colorful characters and the perfectly timed-out moves. I didn't care if it was fake. The music and light shows and the excited crowds made for a silly, but fun, Monday night. Now that I think of it though, wrestling is kind of gross. It's a bunch of sweaty, bulky men in minimal clothing flipping and rolling each other around until someone pretends they have been outdone and taps out. It's kind of weirdly intimate, actually. And it's not a far-off connection to make when thinking of spiritual wrestling. It's an intentional dance between two people who are in tune.

In the months during and after my divorce my spiritual life was growing at full speed. Everything else had halted. My finances. My marriage. My social life. My future plans. Stopped. But I was so thirsty for the Word. I learned truth. I learned the promises that the Bible spoke about, and I was banking on them. However, just because I knew the truth and was attempting to walk in tune with Godly truth, didn't mean I just automatically operated in that knowledge and continued life with ease. No, I had to wrestle down my emotions more often than I care to admit. Fear and sorrow were constantly trying to creep in and take residence. Rejection, futility, and purposelessness attempted to strip any hope I had for, not just my future, but also my children's futures. I had mortal questions like "Why did God let this happen? Why didn't He fix it? Are my children going to be traumatized forever? What do I do now?"

I began to turn those questions directly to God instead of holding them in. This was a newness in my intimacy with Him. Rather than asking, "Why didn't He fix this?", I began to use the word *You*; "Why didn't YOU fix this?" I point-blank asked Him anything and everything. I figured that if He knew what I was thinking already then, I might as well pull out all the stops and speak plainly. The bell had rung, and we were in the ring together. In a strange way, I was actually in the process of more surrendering, letting go of any inhibitions between us.

My shower closet was full of yelling, crying, quiet whispers, and silent listening, and it wasn't rare for me to fall on my knees or even curl up on the tile floor. I was certainly wrestling with God, and I strongly felt His presence. But we never felt like real enemies. That is the difference. Yes, I pushed and pressed Him, but, to this day, those moments are the most intimate and loving that I have ever known.

In Genesis 32, Jacob learned what it meant to wrestle with God. During a journey he learned that his brother Esau, whom he had not seen in many years, was heading his way. This news did not go over well since, in their youth, Jacob had stolen Esau's birthright and blessing. Jacob was now afraid for his life. He had every reason to fear. Esau had previously vowed to kill Jacob over the deceit, and there had not been any communication since, let alone reconciliation. The night before Jacob was to see Esau, Jacob was alone in the dark with his revolving thoughts. Tomorrow he could die under the hands of his brother. He was distraught. An unknown man entered the scene and violently wrestled with Jacob until morning. In verses 24-26 you can see that Jacob seemed to be the aggressor in the match, but at one point the man touched Jacob's hip and dislocated it to subdue him.

> Genesis 32 24-26 *Jacob was left alone, and a man wrestled with him until daybreak.* ²⁵ *When the man saw that He could not defeat him, He struck Jacob's hip socket as they wrestled and dislocated his hip.* ²⁶ *Then He said to Jacob, "Let Me go, for it is daybreak. But Jacob said, "I will not let You go unless You bless me."*

Jacob learned at that second that He had been wrestling with God. He even received a new name; Israel. This name came with a promise for his future and the future of his people. This promise meant that he would be spared when meeting his brother Esau and that there was more to come.

.

> ²⁷ *"What is your name?" the man asked.*

"Jacob," he replied.

²⁸ "Your name will no longer be Jacob," He said. "It will be Israel[b] because you have struggled with God and with men and have prevailed."

God could have eased Jacob's fears in a variety of ways other than wrestling with him. He could have simply just told him not to worry. He could have caused Esau to turn his caravan around. Instead, the God of the universe stepped into Jacob's camp and intimately wrestled with him for hours into the night. I have often wondered what happened in all those hours. What was Jacob saying to the Man all that time? Did he punch him? Grab His hair? Did furniture get smashed and who knows what else? The Bible only uses the word wrestling which leaves the mind to imagine. Whatever happened during that match, God allowed it.

How incredible. God wrestled with man. Jacob stated in verse 30 that he had seen the face of God. Why would God have taken all that time and trouble to physically wrestle with Jacob through his fears? If we look at God's character traits, the answers are there. He is a relational God. He counts it a privilege to be near us, close, intimate, and not just when it's pleasant.

Psalm 34:18 says, *"The Lord is close to the brokenhearted and saves those who are crushed in spirit."*

He also knows that His very presence is a gift. With it comes comfort and peace and confidence in Him. He doesn't want to just shove a few scriptures in front of us and pat us on the back when we are wrestling with our humanity. He wants to wrestle *with* us. When this happens, we get the benefit of His power, His strength, and the assurance that we are not facing our world alone.

We have the mighty and masterful Creator getting sweaty and intimately fighting with us! I sure that God was holding back when wrestling with Jacob. I can't help but think of a loving father wrestling with His toddler son. He could have sat Jacob on his bottom in the dust with a single word or touch of his little finger. Instead, God chose to let Jacob experience Him and when it was time, He showed Jacob a glimpse of His power and therefore His mercy when he dislocated Jacob's hip socket. Jacob's limp became a reminder to him, and the rest of us, of God's intimacy and His power from then on forward.

Jacob knew the truth. Despite his own sin, he was aware that the promises given to his ancestors were flowing through his veins. He knew who God was, and He knew He could count on Him. So did I. By wrestling with God, we are saying to Him, "You exist! I need you! I desire to share my heart and longings with you! I know I cannot do this without You." There is a beautiful surrender here. By inviting God, we are letting go of the idea of fighting this battle on our own. We are declaring to Him that though we know Truth, yet, we are struggling and need His presence. It is a very surrendered, very intimate, part of our sanctification, and, like an intimate wrestling match, it's full of sweaty trust. We are trusting Him with our raw self. No mask. No pretense. Just our limitations allowed to join with His power.

Allowed. He doesn't have to. He wants to.

Isn't it incredible how patient He is with us? God knows the route we need to travel for our brains and heart to line up with Him. Not only was He there with me during my fight to have children, the loss of our twins, the devastation of my marriage, and more, He's always known that it all was going to happen. Yet, He patiently walked with me through every misguided and even sinful decision, ready to catch me when I needed Him.

Some might question then why He didn't stop it all before it happened. While I can't answer that, what I am certain of, and forever grateful for, is that I know Him more intimately because He didn't. God could "zap" anything or anyone into place. He could zap my emotions to straighten out. He could zap my grief to disappear. He could sit me on my bottom and make me listen. He could zap blueprints of my future plans right into my hands. But, He doesn't do that because that is not the best way for us to experience intimacy.

The Bible shows us many times that God acts relationally toward us. Look at the many names listed here and notice how each one alludes to God taking the time to reach and relate to us.

Take some time to think about a few of the intimate names of Jesus by reading the provided scripture and filling out what it says He is.

_____ – *"...who is and who was and who is to come, the Almighty." **Rev. 1:8***

_____– *"I am the Alpha and the Omega, the First and the Last, the Beginning and the End." **Rev. 22:13***

_____ – *"My dear children, I write this to you so that you will not sin. But if anybody does sin, we have an advocate with the Father--Jesus Christ, the Righteous One." **1 John 2:1***

_____– *"Fixing our eyes on Jesus, the author and perfecter of faith, who for the joy set before Him endured the cross, despising the shame, and has sat down at the right hand of the throne of God." **Heb. 12:2***

_____ – *"And Jesus said to them, "Can the wedding guests mourn as long as the bridegroom is with them? The days will come when the bridegroom is taken away from them, and then they will fast." **Matt. 9:15***

_____ – *"And to wait for his Son from heaven, whom he raised from the dead, Jesus who delivers us from the wrath to come." **1 Thess.1:10***

_____- *"I am the good shepherd. The good shepherd lays down his life for the sheep." **John 10:11***

_____– *"...and grant that Your bond-servants may speak Your word with all confidence, while You extend Your hand to heal, and signs and wonders take place through the name of Your holy servant Jesus."* **Acts 4:29-30**

_____ – *"For there is one God, and one mediator between God and men, the man Christ Jesus."* **1 Tim. 2:5**

_____ – *"Jesus said to her, "I am the resurrection and the life. The one who believes in me will live, even though they die."* **John 11:25**

Wonderful _____, **Mighty** _____, **Everlasting** _____, **Prince of** _____ – *"For to us a child is born, to us a son is given, and the government will be on his shoulders. And he will be called Wonderful Counselor, Mighty God, Everlasting Father, Prince of Peace."* **Is. 9:6**

My favorite is "He is the **I Am**". We can surrender to Him, whether in wrestling or in peace, because we know He is **everything** we need.

What do you need to wrestle out with God? If you believe He loves you and that He wants to be part of your wrestling, begin by telling Him here.

_____
_____
_____
_____
_____
_____
_____
_____
_____
_____

CHAPTER 7
Dependence to Surrender

We are functioning in true spiritual dependence when we stop asking if God will show up... again.

The summer after my divorce, I decided to take a road trip from our Florida home back up to Tennessee with the kiddos and visit my best friend from college. It had been a long several months, and, although the days of constant wrestling were starting to fade, frankly, I needed a break. We enjoyed some fun pit stops along the way; I showed them my old college stomping grounds, and we probably enjoyed more laughter and giggles during the whole car ride than in the last year combined. They were 8 and 6 years old and they drank in all the newness. So did I. While staying at my friend's home, I began to feel lighter and even a little rested. It was noticeable. One evening, however, a strangeness came over me. I didn't know if I was coming down with something, so I decided to go lie down in the guest room. I laid there in the silence, and my mind almost seemed to open up into clarity. Within minutes the Holy Spirit helped me narrow down some thoughts that I had not dared to complete since I had arrived. But there it was, plain as day. It was time to move back to Tennessee.

This may not seem like a big deal, but it was. My eyes swelled up with tears. My heart seemed to grow a little just thinking of it, but so did my concerns. I scribbled a long list of obvious barriers that stood in my way of moving. These were legitimate and all-encompassing barriers, such as moving my children from their father, their grandparents, and everything they have ever known. Other than my best friend, I didn't know anyone in this Tennessee town. I had a solid teaching position in Florida, and in Tennessee, there were 400 candidates for every one teaching position available. The list went on. Another concern I had to get answered was that I needed to be sure this was God's desire for us and not mine. This was not a time to be perceived as having a midlife crisis here! Our family had been through so much and moving could not be because I was running away, or just desiring a life change. I had to be 100% sure this was God-ordained. Our entire future was riding on it.

When I came downstairs, the first thing I heard was my son's voice talking on the phone with his dad telling him how much he liked it here in Tennessee and wished he could live here. My jaw dropped open. I simply whispered to the Lord, "If this is You, then you'll make a way."

According to Hebrews 12, God is the Author and Finisher of our faith. He doesn't just write the first few chapters and leave the rest undone. He is a constant. Yet, He knows we need confirmation and reassurance along the way, and, since we are human, He is patient and He loves to prove Himself. When I returned back home from our road trip, I kept my list of barriers near my bed. I prayed that God would either open up a way or shut it down and help me move on. It's funny what happens sometimes when you know you can't make something happen on your own. There is no forcing it, and, because you know that, there is almost a peace. This wasn't on my shoulders. It was on God's.

A few days later I was planning to give away my massive wooden bed to my aunt and uncle. When I took off the mattress and box springs, I noticed a sticker lying on the floor underneath. It was rectangular and traffic cone orange and had large black words printed in the middle which said **DETOUR**. Where in the world did that come from? I had never seen that sticker before and had no idea how long it had been there. I just started laughing.

That weird little sticker filled me with joy. A detour was exactly what was before me.

When we come across a detour sign, if you are anything like me, it's a little unsettling. You don't get to take the route you prepared for or that you know well. It feels a little abrupt to come upon that big orange sign in the middle of the road. You are forced to stop your route and instead, you must go in what seems like a wrong direction. It feels directionless. You start to wonder if it will take longer, if you accidentally miss a sign, and where will you end up? But since you really don't have a choice, you must surrender to go where you are shown. You are dependent on the detour designer.

In the book of Exodus, Moses had to learn surrendered dependence before he was able to lead a nation to be dependent on God. It began when he noticed a bush ablaze. God got his attention with His own detour sign before His voice was even heard, and, when God did speak, He called Moses by name. By the end of the conversation, Moses had been told that God had seen the Jews' suffering and heard their pleas and He wanted Moses to be the one to lead them out of Egypt. God gave him specific instructions, and Moses had several questions.

In Exodus Chapter 3 verse 13, Moses asked God, *"Indeed, when I come to the children of Israel and say to them, 'The God of your fathers has sent me to you,' and they say to me, 'What is His name?' what shall I say to them?* [14] *And God said to Moses, "I AM WHO I AM." And He said, "Thus you shall say to the children of Israel, 'I AM has sent me to you.'"* [15] *Moreover God said to Moses, "Thus you shall say to the children of Israel: 'The Lord God of your fathers, the God of Abraham, the God of Isaac, and the God of Jacob, has sent me to you. This is My name forever, and this is My memorial to all generations.'*

I think one of the reasons we feel insecure about surrendering to detour sign directions is we simply don't trust. However, it's not the actual signs we don't trust. Signs are just signs, wood and metal. What we really struggle with, is trusting the person who put them there. Do they really know what they're doing? Is this really the best way? Do they understand where I am trying to go?

Moses must have known that. Although the idea of leaving Egypt may have been appealing to the enslaved and mistreated Israelites, if he were to convince tens of thousands of people to leave the only place they had ever known and walk into an unknown future, they would have to be sure of WHOM they were relying on for direction and then surrender to Him. Signs are all well and good, but Who is designing and placing them?

Sometimes detours are often there to protect us, but we might not even know from what, so we generate questions. The Israelites did. Would there be enough food? How will Moses know the way? Does a promised land really exist? I cannot begin to imagine the inquiries about this detour. I wonder if they had a "barrier" list like I did. The answer to those and many more questions lie in the name mentioned to Moses; I AM.
I AM.

They are two beautiful words. The words are simple, but absolutely complete. Whatever the Israelites questions were going to be, God already had the answers by pointing to Himself. They didn't have to trust the signs; they could trust the One who laid them out.

Moses began his line of questioning again. The title of Exodus chapter 4 in my version says, *MIRACULOUS SIGNS FOR MOSES*. Even after meeting God, hearing His voice, getting laid-out directions of what was about to happen, Moses still wondered if anyone would believe him. The Lord told Moses in verse 2,

² The Lord asked him, "What is that in your hand?"

"A staff," he replied.

³ Then He said, "Throw it on the ground." He threw it on the ground, and it became a snake. Moses ran from it, ⁴ but the Lord told him, "Stretch out your hand and grab it by the tail." So, he

stretched out his hand and caught it, and it became a staff in his hand. ⁵ "This will take place," He continued, "so they will believe that Yahweh, the God of their fathers, the God of Abraham, the God of Isaac, and the God of Jacob, has appeared to you."

It's easy to judge Moses here because even after a total of three personalized miracles, Moses pleaded with God to choose someone else to go to Pharaoh and lead the Hebrews out of Egypt.

¹⁰ But Moses replied to the Lord, "Please, Lord, I have never been eloquent—either in the past or recently or since You have been speaking to Your servant[c]—because I am slow and hesitant in speech."[d]

¹¹ Yahweh said to him, "Who made the human mouth? Who makes him mute or deaf, seeing or blind? Is it not I, Yahweh? ¹² Now go! I will help[e] you speak and I will teach you what to say."

¹³ Moses said, "Please, Lord, send someone else."[f]

Moses had just witnessed God's power. This was not a matter of deciding if God was powerful enough. Clearly, He was. Yet, Moses was well aware of his own limitations to pull this off, but God didn't want Moses to depend on himself. This was a matter of surrendered dependence, not power. God showed up today; yes, but would God keep showing up or would it be all on "me"?

I get it. For me, there were lots of tangible reasons moving north looked like it was not a viable option, and I knew everyone else around me would think the same. One morning there was a knock at the door. I wasn't expecting company, but I was happy to see one of my sweet friends. This woman was a feisty Cuban from New Jersey who always, with love, told it like it is. She was not a believer, and, when I opened the door, she told me to put on a pot of coffee because we needed to have a talk. We had a very respectful, supportive friendship, even with our spiritual differences. She never had a problem with my speaking freely about my faith, but I made sure I never went beyond an invisible respectful boundary.

She lovingly began her speech by reminding me of all of the

terrible things I had been through and explaining that she just couldn't see any reason I should continue trusting in a God who clearly didn't exist or, if He did, didn't care. I think she was worried about my seriously considering this move, especially since it was based on faith.

Gosh, I loved her for this. She had seen me suffer and barely dog-paddle above water. Her concern was genuine, and it touched me. I could understand how she viewed this. I probably looked foolish or, at the least, naïve. Plus, I had no real evidence to give her that I was on the right track. This indeed looked like a road to more pain, not a protected detour. She wasn't wrong about my suffering, and the end of the long tunnel wasn't in sight. The idea of picking up my kids and moving 600 miles away did seem insane, or even reckless. I had no career to stand on. My husband's financial decisions had put me at square one. At least where I was, all was familiar. The people. My job. Family. Known.

But by the time she had come to my home that morning, God had already knocked off a few barriers from my list. The detour was starting. All I could say to her was that God had shown up and I was surrendering to my faith that He was going to keep showing up and I hoped she'd keep watching.

I don't know where those words came from other than that's all I had to bank on. He *had* to show up.

My favorite part of what I AM said to Moses was toward the end of verse 15 in Chapter 3. *This is My name forever, and this is My memorial to all generations.'*

Wow. His name, **I AM**, is forever. We can count on Him forever. Not just one big show. No. He will always be what we need when He knows we need Him and, if others are really watching, they will see Him show up too. Perfectly and consistently sufficient.

And He was sufficient. The Bible shows us that He showed up

time and time again and the Israelites were released from bondage. As the story goes, they reached the Red Sea and Pharaoh's army was in hot pursuit.

¹⁰ As Pharaoh approached, the Israelites looked up and saw the Egyptians coming after them. Then the Israelites were terrified and cried out to the Lord for help. ¹¹ They said to Moses: "Is it because there are no graves in Egypt that you took us to die in the wilderness? What have you done to us by bringing us out of Egypt? ¹² Isn't this what we told you in Egypt: Leave us alone so that we may serve the Egyptians? It would have been better for us to serve the Egyptians than to die in the wilderness."

¹³ But Moses said to the people, "Don't be afraid. Stand firm and see the Lord's salvation He will provide for you today; for the Egyptians you see today, you will never see again. ¹⁴ The Lord will fight for you; you must be quiet."

The Lord will fight for you. **Hush**. Makes me smile. Let's fast forward to the end result, after the Lord showed up. I want us to imagine our toes standing on the other side of the sea now that the waters had pooled back into place, and the Egyptians had been lost in depths. Take a minute to feel the waters gently lapping on the sand as though nothing was ever amiss. The heaviness of the soldier's battle gear had pulled them to the bottom. The braying of the horses was gone. Chariots had been crushed to pieces from the rushing force of the waves. The great power of the Lord had been on full display, and awe had overcome the crowd. Standing there, they knew His power deserved their dependence.

Exodus 14:31 says, ³¹ When Israel saw the great power that the Lord used against the Egyptians, the people feared the Lord and believed in Him and in His servant Moses.

Sometimes we get to see that kind of power. The Israelites did, at least for a time, and the people began to sing! In chapter 15 verse 13 it says,

> *¹³ "You will lead the people*
> *You have redeemed*
> *with Your faithful love;*
> *You will guide them to Your holy dwelling*
> *with Your strength."*

Within a year, I watched every single barrier on my list crumble. To me, it was no different than the parting of the sea. That is how impossible this list looked to me. By this time, not only was my children's father allowing us to move, he had flown to Tennessee with me to check out schools and neighborhoods and was in full support that this move was beneficial to them long term. I watched the Lord soften his heart, and it was incredible to make this decision as united parents and not just solo. We packed the moving truck, and within the same day, the kids and I pulled into a new state, a new residence, and a new life. My local best friend had told others about our move, and we were greeted with meals and friendship and love. Within 24 hours of being a Tennessean, my children's very own new school offered me a teaching position. My classroom was right next door to my son's. Does a detour get any more personal than that to a momma's heart?

It was all true. He really did show up.

Not only does God want us to trust that we can depend on Him to show up in powerful ways, we can also depend on Him to do so in personal ways. We serve a God who parts massive bodies of water with His might, and yet we also serve a God who gives His people water to quench their thirst.

CHAPTER 7

Just a few days after God's mighty display at the Red Sea the people began to complain that there was no water to drink. I'm sure that God could have prevented their thirst from happening in the first place somehow, but thirst meant that they would have to reconcile with themselves as to whether they would again surrender their trust to God at the first sign of suffering. Moses was annoyed with the people. Take a look at chapter 15 starting at verse 22.

> *²² Then Moses led Israel on from the Red Sea, and they went out to the Wilderness of Shur. They journeyed for three days in the wilderness without finding water. ²³ They came to Marah, but they could not drink the water at Marah because it was bitter—that is why it was named Marah.[f] ²⁴ The people grumbled to Moses, "What are we going to drink?" ²⁵ So he cried out to the Lord, and the Lord showed him a tree. When he threw it into the water,*
>
> *the water became drinkable.*

He showed up again. What is incredible here is that He met their needs, but in a very personally provided way. Verse 27 states, "*²⁷ Then they came to Elim, where there were 12 springs of water and 70 date palms, and they camped there by the waters.*"

According to the scriptures, the Israelites consisted of 12 tribes. Read the above verses again.

Did you catch it? 12 springs. One for each tribe. How beautiful is that?

Again, and Again. He shows up in power and in personal provision!

Yet, at the first sign of trouble, aren't we so similar to these rescued, firsthand-miracle witnesses? Many people refer to the Israelites as an analogy to how easily we forget what God does for us. Yes, that may be true. However, I think there is something more troubling. I think our grumbling, complaining and worry when we face a trial in our lives isn't because we forget. I think it's actually that we haven't reached a consistent pattern of dependence on the Lord because we wonder if he will show up yet *again*. When we grumble, we question His continued provision.

This book is all about surrender, as you have seen chapter after chapter. That is our part. Choosing to believe that God will continue to show up is a sign of maturing faith and dependence on Him. It's realizing that He doesn't ever reach some "show up" quota and disappear. We won't run out of opportunities to see Him move in and around us and before us. You're not going to forget what He does for you, but most importantly, He's not going to forget YOU. He will show up, again. Surrender to that dependent truth. Just you watch.

Read Exodus 6:1-9

On the lines below, write down the promises that God states after each time He says the word WILL.

_____
_____
_____
_____
_____
_____
_____
_____

How many times did He say the word WILL? _____

Move over to chapter 15 and read the Israelites song.

Did He fulfill His promises? _____

Was the Lord worth of the Israelites surrendered dependence? _____

In what ways does the Lord want you to depend on Him?
_____
_____

CHAPTER 8
Waiting to Surrender

Waiting is not for the passive or faint of heart. It is an active surrender with open hands and walking feet that are willing to change direction.

With great intentions, people often share trite phrases with others like, "If it's meant to be, it will be easy" or similar clichés. I can see the general meaning of a statement like that. It's also a comforting thought for someone who wonders if they made the right decision. While I don't want to completely pick that phrase apart, I'd like to shed a little Biblical light on it. The word easy alludes to several different connotations for people such as "if it were meant to be, then it will be...simple, streamlined, require little effort, second nature", etc. When God reveals a plan or direction, I'm not sold on it needing to be easy in order to be "meant to be". Certainly, it can be, but it also depends on your own idea of what is easy.

There are plenty of examples in the Bible that were "meant to be" that would support both being easy and being very difficult. Rahab simply let down a red cord from her window to escape destruction. Daniel prayed in the lion's den and was spared. Shadrach, Meshach and Abednego just had to stand there, and the flames didn't consume them.

So, as far as *endurance-required* actions go, these examples seem to show that the end result was pretty "easy" to get to.

But, what about when Rahab sat near her window waiting to see the army of God appear on the horizon? Did she fight worry and fear that they would forget her or that she'd be found out? Was that easy? When Daniel was lowered into the darkness and could smell the lions' breath and see the glint bouncing off their teeth, was that easy? When the three young boys watched the soldiers heat up the furnace, did their hearts race, and did they imagine the pain of being burnt alive? Was that easy?

Think about the walls of Jericho. The walls fell once Joshua and his people marched around it as directed. In comparison to attacking miles of stone and rock with ancient sledgehammers, walking seems pretty easy. But it did require an enormous amount of what looked like foolish faith for several days. It required holding fast to an impossible promise that this city would be theirs. I have found that anything that is meant to be has quite a variance of ease and difficulty. Sometimes the variance is external and sometimes internal. I'm not convinced that ease is required to confirm that something is meant to be, but I do believe that God has a way of showing us how He orchestrates what is meant to be through events and people and that He does not require us to force His plan to happen.

My kids and I used the summer we moved to Tennessee to play. We needed it. We explored the surrounding areas and created new friendships, and I think we were all in awe of how quickly we were feeling at home. I was able to be fully invested in the moment. This was new. I felt a calming and peaceful refreshment. But it wasn't easy. I had left my parents in Florida. I was starting a new job soon. My kids were entering new schools. I didn't know where anything was in town. All the typical moving "to dos" needed to be done like finding a local bank, insurance, buying winter clothes (that was very new), forwarding mail, going house hunting etc. It's not that those things were difficult, but I had to be an active participant in this new plan that I was in.

I also wondered so many things. Would I connect with people I worked with? Would my kids make Godly friends?

Which church should we attend? Should I start dating? (That one was terrifying to think of.) How will I do this single mom thing away from all of my family? Although moving to Tennessee offered the answers to many questions I had had in Florida, it also opened the door to many new questions, and most of the answers were not going to come quickly.

I haven't met a person yet who enjoys waiting for answers. We all want to know if what we are waiting for will work out for our benefit. That's what it really comes down to. Whatever the question is, the anticipation is only annoying because we don't know if we will like or dislike the answer. Waiting seems to be a theme in my life. I am certain my personal God knew that I have needed to develop qualities that naturally and supernaturally come through waiting, especially when I choose to surrender the answers to Him. What I am also learning is that God doesn't just want us to surrender the answers; He also wants us to surrender the anticipation.

I used to think waiting was something that only meek and quiet people were good at. Those characteristics must have run out when it was my turn to receive them, so they aren't natural for me. The excitement and the relief I was finally feeling when I moved to Tennessee was intoxicating. If you have ever been functioning in a dark space in your life and have experienced the first sense of light, you can't help but want to run to it. I picture a scuba diver lost in the black caverns of a deep freshwater spring, disoriented, and panicked, and running out of air.

Can you feel the overwhelming sense of gratitude and joy at the first sight of light, knowing the break of the surface wasn't far? This is the relief I felt. I could exhale.

For a few recent years I had had very limited options. As a matter of fact, most choices had been made for me. I had lost my twins, my husband, my home, my friend group, my family of in-laws, and, out of necessity rather than choice, I had returned to teaching. When I moved, all of a sudden, there were not only a million questions, there were a million options too! We were temporarily living in an apartment, and when it came time to consider house hunting, I didn't have a clue where to start. When I wasn't teaching, how would I fill my time? I wasn't even sure I knew what interested me. I wasn't bouncing my life or options off someone else anymore. I had a blank canvas in front of me, and I had no idea what the rest of my life could be. For so long I had been surviving. But now I was starting to wonder what thriving looks like.

The one thing that I did know is this: I wanted to go, be, do, whatever God wanted. I had seen His mighty hand in my life. I had felt His personal affection for me. He had indeed shown up. My faith in His delight in my life was my new foundation for whatever was next, I felt confident that His way was what I wanted.

Sometimes, the answers came quickly. A friend told me about a house on a few acres that seemed like a dream. It didn't come easy, but it did fall into place. There is no doubt this home was a gift from God. Meant to be. It needed a lot of work, but at least I could afford to buy it. It needed a lot of maintenance, but the three of us tackled it. My children and I grew in so many ways at that home. We learned how to work power tools and fix things. We met neighbors who took us on like their own little family and helped us. We planted a huge garden, got chickens and barn cats, tore out carpet, demolished and rebuilt a kitchen, got scrapes and cuts and stitches, landscaped, refinished and sold furniture for extra cash, and we healed together as a new little family there.

The rest of our lives were not planned out. We were living day-to-day at this point, and it was in the anticipation of what the rest of our lives were going to be like that we chose to enjoy the daily moments. We were active in those daily moments. Our hands were open to the unknown, and so were our hearts. We didn't sit there and wait for our new life to happen, but we didn't force it either. We were learning to actively wait with a peaceful and surrendered anticipation. Learning.

This passage hit me between the eyes, and, when we walk through it together, it might surprise you too.

Psalms 130:5-6 "I wait for the LORD, my soul waits, and in his Word, I hope; my soul waits for the Lord more than watchmen for the morning, more than watchmen for the morning."

The Hebrew word for "wait" in the above verse as well as several well-known "wait" verses is **Qavah**, meaning to "look for, hope, expect." Qavah is a verb. When this word is used in the scriptures, it refers to an active waiting. It is not a passive waiting whatsoever. This is a confident expectation and even a demand from God that is rooted in the knowledge that God is faithful and constantly at work and we don't want to miss it.

Look at how the Psalmist repeated the last line to make a clear analogy. Imagine the watchmen above staying up all night, squinting their eyes at the distance, downing coffee, anticipating the first glint of the sunrise along the horizon so their waiting could rest. When God shows up, we can rest in His answer and direction. To wait for Yahweh means to eagerly hope for, seek, and expect Him!

Yes, yes, I might know what you are thinking... "be still and know He is God". If you read the entire passage that comes from Psalm 46, the Lord is actively saving His people and He is saying "I've got this. Just **watch** Me do my thing and try not to get in the way".

Yes, be still- but *WATCH!* We might not think of watching being an action, but it is. As a matter of fact, I think it requires great restraint and faith to do it well!

So, this kind of active waiting is also not referring to meddling or manipulating an outcome, but it also doesn't mean putting life on hold or sitting back and demanding for God to make the dreams and whims of our hearts come to life. It is a holy, obedient surrender, spending time in His presence and HIs Word, pursuing what is Godly in our daily choices, trusting our feelings to catch up, and knowing God is moving whether we see it or not.

It's being ready. We don't move forward without His directions, but we don't take a hibernating nap either.

Active waiting occurs in many places throughout the Bible. The actions during the anticipation are actions of faith and fortitude. While, yes, there are times when being still was required, the results of the stories below would have turned out completely differently had the main characters chosen passivity while they waited.

Ruth: After her husband died, she followed and cared for her mother-in-law and gleaned grain to help them survive, and soon King Boaz noticed her character.

(What if she didn't?)

Prodigal son's father: He didn't write off his rebellious son as was the tradition and the cultural expectation. Instead he watched down the road for his return and was ready to celebrate, believing his son would come home.

(What if he didn't?)

Hosea: He repeatedly gave his love to his unfaithful wife, retrieving her over and over, while his heart was desperately wanting her love and faithfulness. His example spoke to the nation of Israel in a real and tangible way as a result of his active waiting.

(What if he didn't?)

Abraham: He declared to his son that God would send a sacrifice and he walked up the mountain in obedience prepared to prove his dedication even while believing he wouldn't have to.

(What if he didn't?)

Rahab: She held to her promise and the truth that the God she heard about would conquer her city. While she waited, she watched for the exact moment to let down the red cord and trusted she would be remembered and saved. She was eventually a mother in the line of Jesus.

(What if she didn't?)

Paul: He was in prison and could have just sat there waiting for death. With no reason to think he would be rescued; he sang praises behind bars and shared the gospel. Thew prison doors flew open.

(What if he didn't?)

Esther: Through faith she risked her life by boldly entering the King's presence without an invitation, an action punishable by death, to ask him to save her people, hoping God would intervene. She waited for the right time. And he did.

(What if she didn't?)

Woman with the blood illness: She didn't sit in her home just wanting healing. She risked the opinion of others in public to seek healing through faith by touching the hem of Jesus's robe and awaited an expected healing.

(What if she didn't?)

Noah: He trusted God for decades that rain was real and was coming even though he had never seen it. He didn't wait for proof. He got busy and began a life-long project that saved his family while he waited for rain.

(What if he didn't?)

Waiting isn't terribly pleasant. Sometimes it can feel worse than the answer we wait for. Waiting and I know each other very well. We are not best friends, but we are necessary co-workers. Waiting for a year for my husband to determine he no longer wanted to be my husband was torture. Waiting for my twins to be born only to pass away was a nightmare. Waiting is not the precursor to getting everything we want, but sometimes it is a precursor to the growth we need and a developing dependence. So, don't misunderstand my intent. In no way am I implying in this chapter that, just because waiting is active, that it's any less of a trial. When, however, we spend so much of our lives waiting for the answer, we risk missing out on the work God is doing within the anticipation. Before the answer comes, actively pursue the Lord. This is how you grow in the waiting. Surrender your focus away from obtaining the answer or reaching the end of the waiting because that focus can steal the day-to-day intimacy the Lord desires with you in the meantime.

If you're wondering how you can actively surrender your waiting, start by answering these questions.

Are you worshiping while you wait? _____

1 Chronicles 16:23-21

Are you grateful while you wait? _____

Romans 11:36

Are you knocking on doors or pushing them? _____

Psalm 16:2

Are you worried while your wait?_____

Isaiah 41:10

Are you inviting trusted Christian friends/family to pray for you? _____

1 Timothy 2:1

Are you in prayer?_____

Psalm 63:1

Is your joy diminished while you are waiting? _____

1 Thessalonians 5:16-18

CHAPTER 9
Heart to Surrender

Allowing an unsurrendered heart to lead is about as wise as putting a leash on a wild lion.

During the last few years of healing, rebuilding, waiting, and seeking the Lord for our future, I felt like I was fully awake. I didn't want to miss an important moment or take anything for granted. My spiritual ears were becoming more in tune to the Spirit, and my spiritual eyes were recognizing God's hand in the world around me. I began to pray for God to tune my heart.

I wanted to want what He wanted. The trust was there. Now I needed to grow my desires into His. If the God I served was good, then I wanted to learn to abandon my human tendency to lean toward human tendencies. My heart was healing, and it became clear to me that this new heart had to stay in surrender to His heart if my future was to be in His hands.

We use the word *heart* quite often in our language. Certainly, a word that is nearly overused is easy to define, right? Common phrases we use almost make the HEART a cliche', and we tend to accept this familiarity as truth without really having a clear understanding. When we speak these phrases below, what do we actually mean? If we don't know what the heart is, are these phrases truth, arbitrary, even *dangerous*?

Follow your heart. (What is the heart so I can follow it? and should I?)

The heart wants what the heart wants. (How does it want?)

You have a big heart. (A big what?)

Heart of stone. (This sounds like emotions- isn't that brain stuff?)

Home is where the heart is. (Feelings again?)

Heart*ache*. (Hurt Feelings?)

Get to the heart of it. (Understanding?)

I've had a change of heart (Mind? Desire?)

My heart isn't in it (Choice? Will? Desire?)

Wear your heart on your sleeve (Our feelings? Our identity?)

You are close to my heart (Connected feelings?)

Heart to heart talk (Sharing thoughts/feelings with each other?)

So, which one is it? *Feelings? Thoughts? Desires?*

The Bible mentions the heart almost 1,000 times. It must be important. If it is this important, then we ought to prevent loose language from confusing or diminishing its real meaning. The truth sets us free, so, if we FULLY understand the meaning of *heart* then it completely changes and deepens the meanings of the phrases, but, more importantly, the scripture we learn concerning the heart becomes truly applicable.

English is a combination of several languages, which is neat because we get many words to express even one thought. The accompanying problem is that we can miss the specific intention of a word in connection to scripture.

Greek and Hebrew words are very specific. For example, the origin of the word *heart* in the Greek language is "kardia", which means "control center" holding the intellect, emotions, and will.

In Hebrew, the word *heart* is "leb" meaning the mind, will, and the seat of courage (emotion).

These meanings show us the heart is *not* one thing! This blew my mind! Its usage is not different than if I used the word *puzzle*. You know that when we say puzzle, we don't mean one thing. We mean a multi-piece picture that is incomplete without all of its components. You know that feeling when you've worked for hours to fit each piece only to find out at the end that a piece is missing? It feels terrible! You can't enjoy the rest of the 999 pieces until that one last piece is found. So, it is with the heart. God did not intend it to be a complete and functioning picture without each connected piece.

Now, take a minute to reread the phrases above and see how this new knowledge affects the meanings.

Everyone has a three-piece heart, Christians and non-Christians alike. When we accept Christ, we are given the Holy Spirit moving among the heart like a soft-spoken fuzzy haired public television painter. He is gentle and intentional in his ability to paint a new landscape on our heart puzzle. The Bible shows us how the human picture our heart puzzle makes is dark, deceitful, and ugly -- something we'd want to hide. When we allow the Word of God's bright colors to wash over our heart and the Holy Spirit the chance to create a masterpiece, our puzzle becomes a unique work of art that stands out and shouts His talents.

In keeping with the understanding of our new multiple-piece heart puzzle, let's see what the Bible says about it (emotions, mind, will). How do these verses have new meaning? Is your heart surrendered?

Proverbs 4:23 Above all else, guard your heart **(emotions, mind, will)**, *for everything you do flows from it.*

Jeremiah 29:13 You will seek me and find me when you seek me with all your heart **(emotions, mind, will)**.

Psalm 51:10 Create in me a pure heart **(emotions, mind, will)**, *O God, and renew a steadfast spirit within me.*

Psalm 19:14 *May these words of my mouth and this meditation of my heart* **(emotions, mind, will)** *be pleasing in your sight, Lord, my Rock and my Redeemer.*

Ezekiel 36:26 And I will give you a new heart **(emotions, mind, will)**, *and a new spirit I will put within you. And I will remove the heart* **(emotions, mind, will)** *of stone from your flesh and give you a heart* **(emotions, mind, will)** *of* flesh.

Proverbs 21:2 Every way of a man is right in his own eyes, but the Lord weighs the heart **(emotions, mind, will)**.

James 4:8 Draw near to God, and he will draw near to you. Cleanse your hands, you sinners, and purify your hearts **(emotions, mind, will)**, *you double-minded.*

Psalm 112:7 He is not afraid of bad news; his heart **(emotions, mind, will)** *is firm, trusting in the Lord.*

Jeremiah 17:9-10 The heart **(emotions, mind, will)** *is deceitful above all things, and desperately sick; who can understand it? "I the Lord search the heart* **(emotions, mind, will)** *and test the mind, to give every man according to his ways, according to the fruit of his deeds."*

Proverbs 17:22 A joyful heart **(emotions, mind, will)** *is good medicine, but a crushed spirit dries up the bones.*

Proverbs 14:30 A tranquil heart **(emotions, mind, will)** *gives life to the flesh, but envy makes the bones rot.*

Proverbs 27:19 As in water face reflects face, so the heart **(emotions, mind, will)** *of man reflects the man.*

This is just a snapshot!

So, how do we surrender the *parts* of our heart?

Understanding that the heart is actually three things (emotions, mind, and will), and knowing that the Bible tells us we have control of our heart, means we have control over these three things. Nowhere does it claim that control is easy. Concerning emotions, there are plenty of examples of Godly men and women who wrestled and gave in to their emotions. How about Sampson and his lustful desire for Delilah? Moses when he came down from the mountain with the first set of commandments and saw the idol worship happening among his people? David's Desire for Bathsheba and his killing her husband? Eve and her distrust of what God had said that led her to eating and sharing the forbidden fruit? Cain's jealousy which led to his killing his brother Abel?

Every situation above began with an unchecked emotion that eventually spun out of control. And every situation above eventually led to a consequence.

We have to identify the emotion and its potential harm. Emotions are a gift from God. He experiences emotion. He doesn't command us to never feel anything. But emotions are meant to do two things.... Point and Prod.

They are an alert for us to see our sinful desires that come out during certain times. They are to point out the places within our heart that still need God's sifting. They are meant to show us what we are still trying to control. But they are also there to indicate what we cherish, both good and bad.

Emotions also prod us either toward God or away from Him. When we are seeking God's ways in our life, our emotions should move us into actions that look like Him. When we feel anger, do our actions attack or forgive? When there is a real reason to be afraid, do we sit in that fear or invite God and trust He's not afraid. When sadness floods in, do we isolate? Are our words hopeless in that sadness or hopeful in the Creator? Do we drink up scripture knowing that there is life within, or do we seek earthly means of temporary comfort?

There's good news. It's not all on you. God knew we would struggle with this. He's not expecting you to get this right *without* Him. We need Him. We have a tendency to FEED the emotion we FEEL and FEEL the emotion we FEED. He knows that. It's like craving sugar makes us eat sugar which makes us crave sugar. It's a cycle, and if we don't set up preventions, we will fall in an emotional spinny-ride that gets us nowhere fast.

Proverbs 16:32 Better a patient person than a warrior, one with self-control than one who takes a city.

Look at that! God is stating that we are *more powerful* and *more than a conqueror* when we learn how to win the battle of self-control. Self-control starts with controlling emotions (not ignoring or eliminating them). Actions don't just happen out of nowhere. The actions are what produces consequences, so by inviting God to teach us how to control our emotions, we actually STOP a painful battle.

The second piece of surrendering our heart is disciplining our mind. It's the decision factory! As humans, we are pretty good at gathering intel, weighing the consequences of all of our options, and considering how our choices will affect others. But we don't like it so much when we realize our decisions produce regret so sometimes when we do silly things. I think that's why we look for "signs". In my experience though, tarot cards, eeny meeny miny, and Jesus's picture on burnt toast aren't the best ways to make up our minds.

Lots of people struggle with decision making and would absolutely love it if their toast showed them the way. Why? If a sign, or even the basic gathering of facts, made it crystal clear what we should do, then we wouldn't fear regret. The blame of the wrong choice wouldn't be on us.

But. We *are* the ones responsible for our choices, not our toast.

Think about the phrase "*make up your mind*". We know that it means to decide. But really it means something far more important than the decision itself and it starts before the choice is to be made.

It's back to the basic idea of garbage in, garbage out. What is our mind made up *of*? When we are faced with decisions, have we invested in studying the Word? What about listening to worship music which changes our focus from ourselves to God? How about surrounding ourselves with encouraging friends? Have we challenged our brain to retrain its sinful and human way of thinking over time, or have we given in to it over and over? We make hundreds of choices every day, and each choice is connected in some way to what is already in our brain!

What we eat. (healthy/ unhealthy)

What we wear. (perception of ourselves)

What we say (out of the abundance of the heart the mouth speaks)

What we watch, laugh at, talk about, purchase, think about, desire, worry about etc...

So, who is in charge of what is in our brain? Satan does throw darts of lies at our mind, but he cannot read our minds. God can. God understands the inner workings of our brain, and the parts that have tendencies to think opposite of Him. When we give Him control of our thoughts, He can target the weak areas and strengthen them with truth. But this is a constant battle. Satan will never give up on attacking your mind. God will never give up on filling it with truth to defend it. Our sole job in this battle is letting God have the fight by not entertaining the lies of the enemy and by seeking truth and investing time in what is holy.

Romans 1 speaks of repeated sin being a cause for a corrupted mind. The words are very literal in translation, and they point to the fact that our brain can be rewired. So, if sin can rewire a brain's neural pathways to easily slip into sinful thinking, then isn't it true that God's truth in word and action can rewire our brains to then more easily make Godly decisions?

When trials come and stress is thick, the baby is crying, the bills are piling, sickness is real, and nothing seems fair, this is when we really find out what our mind is made of.

The third part of the heart is our will. I wrote about the emotions and the mind first because, without those in daily surrender, is it possible to surrender our will? This is where we generate our desires and ultimately our actions. When we feel and think compassionately, we act compassionately. When we feel and think lovingly, humbly, joyfully, patiently, that is how we act. It is no accident that the will is a major piece of the heart puzzle, but I believe it naturally functions as a result of surrendering the first two pieces. Our surrender through our actions is truly the revealer of the heart. *Do we really want what God wants?*

I have found in the last few years that scripture memory has been a consistent means of surrender for me. I am not a natural memorizer, but when I do hide His word in my heart the meanings and application become more alive in connected situations, and it has built my confidence in the truth it brings.

Take a look at the scriptures below. Instead of filling anything out this time, choose one verse each week over the next few weeks and commit them to memory as an act of surrendering your heart.

Romans 12:2 Do not conform to the pattern of this world but be transformed by the renewing of your mind. Then you will be able to test and approve what God's will is—his good, pleasing and perfect will.

2 Corinthians 11:3 But I am afraid that just as Eve was deceived by the serpent's cunning, your minds may somehow be led astray from your sincere and pure devotion to Christ.

Colossians 3:2 Set your minds on things above, not on earthly things.

Proverbs 4:23 Above all else, guard your heart, for everything you do flows from it.

Ephesians 4:23 Instead, let the Spirit renew your thoughts and attitudes.

CHAPTER 10
Satisfaction of Surrender

It's far easier to give up your right to be right when you realize that His right will always satisfy you more than your right.

In the previous chapters, we have seen primary examples of the Lord leading His people toward surrender in several different ways. Not long ago I was in conversation with someone who was hanging on to a toxic relationship. It was clearly aging this person by the second. I could see them fighting with themselves over breaking it off, being free of the toxicity, and yet yearning for things to change for the better if they just hoped a little longer. Wisdom said run. I could tell that they knew it. So, n this conversation, I told them that it seemed they knew what they should do, and they replied, "Yeah, yeah I know. Surrender." Even with all of the examples I've given in this book, we have a tendency to hang our heads and accept surrender as a form of defeat. What I want to leave you with is the exact opposite.

Where in the Bible did God ask anyone to give up something and then receive something harmful, or even of lesser value? Nowhere.

Where in the Bible did God call someone to a difficult situation and leave them on their own? Nowhere.

Where in the Bible did God not have a plan? Nowhere.

Where in the Bible did a person mess up and God had no idea how to fix it, bring something good from it, use it to teach that person and others, and bring glory to Him anyway? Nowhere.

> *Isaiah 30:18 Therefore the Lord longs to be gracious to you,*
> *And therefore He waits on high to have compassion on you.*
> *For the Lord is a God of justice;*
> *How blessed are all those who long for Him.*

God is good. When we grasp these three words to the fullest extent that our minds are capable of grasping, it changes how we view surrender. If God is only good, then everything He *longs* to do for us and with us is only good. That means that surrendering to Him in every way, shape, and form is good for us. Surrender is not defeat. I want you to imagine yourself in an army uniform standing over a large unrolled map on a table in the official battle strategist's tent near a battlefield. Your officers are waiting for your instructions on how to proceed. This is your first time in this position and you truly want to prove yourself and do right by your regiment. There are men out there ready to fight, and their lives are in your hands. You have surveyed the topography as best you could. You have poured over the intelligence you've gathered. The time is near, and it's all on your shoulders. You have made your decisions, drawn out the plans of attack, and, just when you were about to call in the officers to deliver the orders, an unexpected soldier enters the tent. Not just any soldier. A 5 star general. His face is weathered from years of experience, but his eyes are steady. He stands tall and broad and he is holding something. He tells you that he knows how to win this battle. He knows the enemy's plans. He knows the strengths of your army and the idiosyncrasies of the terrain not detailed on the map you hold. He's fought battles here before, many times. He has never lost. He promises that if you hand over your plans and allow him to lead the battle, you will win. The catch is, you don't get to see the plans before you make your decision. What would you do?

I dare say that after all of the work put into a battle strategy, it may be a little tough to toss it. It means you don't get to lead your men. It means all the energy you spent worrying and gathering intel doesn't get translated into anything further. It means stepping back and giving up the lead. Your choice here is surrender and win or continue control and hope for the best.

Do we really believe that God is good? Do we really believe He knows best and that we will be fully satisfied with what *He* wants for us? We struggle so much with this because we really think we know what we want sometimes. We seem to think that what God wants for us is only good for us and not going to be something we will actually like or desire.

Is that what we boil God down to? A dad forcing us to eat a plate of broccoli for the rest of our lives because it's good for us? Dear friends, if that is you, I have good news! The plans He has for you cannot be reduced to only what is good for us. That's just part of it. When we choose a life of daily and repeated surrender, set on a foundation of confidence and excitement for what God has in store, we don't just get what is good for us; we get all of His fulfilled promises.

It has been several years now since I've moved to Tennessee. I have seen first-hand His promises. I do not believe in the "prosperity gospel" that some latch onto because of what they hope to gain; let's get that straight when we talk about promises. That is surface-level stuff, and I would be so sad if that is all any of us are seeking because there is so much more satisfaction to be had in HIM rather than in our spoiled circumstances. We've got to get beyond the earthly riches and a sought-after easy Christian life as tangible evidence of God's blessings and presence. In our truly surrendered lives, we will not miss out on the *real depths* His Kingdom has to offer.

In these years, there have been plenty of ups and downs. I have experienced successes, joy, growth, financial recovery, beautiful new memories, emotional healing, a new career, and deep friendships, and I have even come to treasure a mutually forgiven co-parenting relationship with my ex-husband. Praise the Lord!

I've also faced trials, losses, grief, uncertainty, hurt, pain, and disappointment. I think it's important to note the struggles along with the successes. Nothing negative negates the positive because it's all in God's hands working together for the good as He promises. It doesn't make me question His leading me here. If anything, my facing challenges gives God a continued opportunity to satisfy my choice to surrender by continuing to show up and prove Himself again and again.

He really loves doing that.

So, what are His promises? When we live a surrendered and trust that He is good, what do we have to look forward to? This is about to get exciting!

1) When you surrender and choose to stop relying on yourself, but to rely on God's goodness, contentment enters the scene. Look at Philippians.

Philippians 4:11-13

11 I don't say this out of need, for I have learned to be content in whatever circumstances I am. 12 I know both how to have a little, and I know how to have a lot. In any and all circumstances I have learned the secret of being content—whether well fed or hungry, whether in abundance or in need. 13 I am able to do all things through Him[a] who strengthens me.

God's strength and all of His character begins to flow through you! Think back to the previous themes of these chapters and see how God's promises are fulfilled in scripture when we rely on Him for our contentment.

2) When we are searching for comfort and choose to give Him

control, God promises...

Isaiah 55:8-9

*⁸ "For My thoughts are not your thoughts,
and your ways are not My ways."
This is the Lord's declaration.
9 "For as heaven is higher than earth,
so My ways are higher than your ways,
and My thoughts than your thoughts.*

3) When we are sick and in pain and we choose to seek Him through it, He promises...

"So do not fear, for I am with you; do not be dismayed, for I am your God. I will strengthen you and help you; I will uphold you with my righteous right hand." Isaiah 41:10

4) When we suffer loss and grief and trust His eternal perspective, He promises...

The LORD is close to the brokenhearted and saves those who are crushed in spirit. Psalm 34:18

5) When we are injured and betrayed, yet we surrender our rights to be justified and instead face our own sin, He promises...

, 3 ᶠBlessed be the ᵍGod and Father of our Lord Jesus Christ, the Father of mercies and ʰGod of all comfort, 4 ⁱwho comforts us in all our affliction, so that we may be able to comfort those who are in any affliction, with the comfort with which we ourselves are comforted by God. **2 Corinthians 1:3-4**

6) When we invite Him to wrestle with us and we seek His presence in our concerns, He promises...

Draw near to God, and He will draw near to you. James 4:8

7) When we reject the ideology of independent living and surrender to dependence on God, He promises...

> *It is not that we are competent in[a] ourselves to consider anything as coming from ourselves, but our competence is from God.   2Corinthians 3:5*

8) When we choose to wait and surrender our tendency to push God into action, He promises...

> *We wait for Yahweh;*
> *He is our help and shield.*
> *21 For our hearts rejoice in Him*
> *because we trust in His holy name.*
> *22 May Your faithful love rest on us, Yahweh,*
> *for we put our hope in You.*
>
> *Psalm 33:20-22*

9) When we surrender our hearts and allow God to transform us, He promises...

> *And we all, who with unveiled faces contemplate the Lord's glory, are being transformed into his image with ever-increasing glory, which comes from the Lord, who is the Spirit. 2 Corinthians 3:18*
>
> *Do not conform to the pattern of this world, but be transformed by the renewing of your mind. Then you will be able to test and approve what God's will is—his good, pleasing and perfect will. Romans 12:2*

    While I do not know what tomorrow brings, the confidence that has boiled and solidified within me through my surrender and His consistency allows me to end this book unfinished, but totally satisfied. There doesn't have to be a romanticized ending where I tell you how the story wraps up just right. I don't need to put a period here concerning my earthly circumstances because eternally, it is finished. I know the Author loves me and I wouldn't need to continue surrendering if I already knew the end. But He does and it is good. It is all worked out for His glory.

When you finish this book, I ask you to do two things:

First: Start studying His promises. There are so many beyond the few I have listed here. Understanding the character of God through what He promises us helps us recognize how faithful He is when we surrender.

Second: Jot down the moments He shows up when you chose to get out of the way. Build your trust in Him by acknowledging when His words prove true. Eagerly anticipate Him to do what He says, but you must know what He says in the first place.

You can't lose. Surrendering is an act of trust with a guaranteed result of eternal satisfaction. If we can surrender how we feel and think about surrender from a weary and drudgery act to a prize-winning opportunity, the lens that we see everything through from now on changes! We get to go from worry to exciting anticipation. From fear to confidence.

From frowning at the past to laughing at the future no matter what highs or lows it brings because now we know the secret and have experienced the Satisfaction of Surrender is all about Him.

ABOUT THE AUTHOR

Megan J. Marasigan

Megan is a teacher and writer. She is currently studying Biblical counseling. She resides in Tennessee with her family and close friends and attends a local Bible based church in Nashville. She loves digging into the Word, which inspires her writing and reaching others for Christ.

Made in the USA
Columbia, SC
07 September 2020